COACHING YOUTH RUGBY

An Essential Guide for Coaches, Parents and Teachers

COACHING YOUTH RUGBY

An Essential Guide for Coaches, Parents and Teachers

Keith Richardson

THE CROWOOD PRESS

First published in 2014 by
The Crowood Press Ltd
Ramsbury, Marlborough
Wiltshire SN8 2HR

www.crowood.com

This impression 2016

British Library Cataloguing-in-Publication Data
A catalogue record for this book is available from the British Library.

ISBN 978 1 84797 611 6

Acknowledgements
Thank you to the following for their help and support in the preparation of this
book: Martin Kimber, Wycliffe College; Julian Brammer, Haileybury; Dave Spencer,
Stroud Rugby Club; Mark Nicholson, Marling School; Hartpury College Rugby
Club; Simon Lane, Gloucester Rugby; Ian Smith, RFU L4 coach; Tom Burwell.

Note
Throughout this book, the pronoun 'he' has been used for the sake of
convenience. However, the author and publishers would like to point out that all
the activities in this book are equally applicable to both male and female players.

Typeset by Jean Cussons Typesetting, Diss, Norfolk

Printed and bound in Malaysia by Times Offset (M) Sdn Bhd

CONTENTS

PREFACE

Coaching Youth Rugby serves as a guide for those just starting out coaching young rugby players, as well as seasoned coaches who are dealing with players after non-contact rugby. In addition to helping teach fundamental rugby skills and plan enjoyable coaching sessions, *Coaching Youth Rugby* presents field-tested, age-specific coaching information to help coaches learn how to communicate with players, parents, other coaches and officials. It will also teach coaches how to manage their team on match days, including measures to provide for safety and for administering basic first aid.

Whatever their experience or aspirations, this book will enable readers to fulfil the responsibility of all youth, age group and adult rugby coaches: to nurture and develop the young athletes who are the future of rugby, and to develop sound coaching knowledge for when those young players develop.

KEY TO THE SYMBOLS USED IN THIS BOOK

CONE

ATTACKER

DEFENDER

DIRECTION OF RUN

DIRECTION OF PASS

BALL

TAGS

POLES

TACKLE SHIELD (HAND HELD)

TACKLE BAG (SAUSAGE BAG)

GOAL POSTS

WHEELED SCRUM (ANTI-CLOCKWISE)

LEVEL SCRUM

INTRODUCTION: LET THE GAME BE THE TEACHER

'We'll soon coach that out of him!'

I was once helping out at a coaching holiday course, and a game of touch was going on with one group – and we all (the coaches, anyway) simply had to stop what we were doing to watch what was unfolding before our eyes. One of the young players was dazzling – he simply hypnotized the opposition, and continually made breaks, then fed his team with exquisite passes. It was a master class in what the running game was all about – and then a fellow coach next to me came out with the immortal 'We'll soon coach that out of him!'

This coach was not, however, a disciple of contact rugby – of grinding, forward-dominated rugby that is developed from drills-based coaching; he was, and is, an exponent of attacking with ball in hand, and he is very gifted in developing and nurturing players' running, handling and passing skills. Unfortunately he might have put his finger on a serious problem in *how* rugby is introduced and coached in the early stages.

When I was a young teacher I watched two Welsh schoolmasters 'introduce' young players to rugby. The organization was superb, and the technical knowledge imparted was impressive, and the boys soon found out all about the skill of passing this oddly shaped ball. But they were sitting down in very strictly controlled lines of four, and it took forever for the teachers to let them run and handle – and even then, the activity was constantly stopping so that a technical point could be made by Sir(s).

This may not have put the pupils off the game forever, but it must have served to imprint on their early awareness that the game is all about organization, straight lines and instruction – when actually it isn't. Even the best organized drill session tends to come to a shuddering halt when some poor player passes badly and/or drops the ball – and the majority are then waiting around again instead of being active.

Another coaching memory still makes me cringe: I, a coach with a fair amount of experience of coaching at the top end of the game, had been invited to take part in a rugby day for very young players, and the eager-eyed boys and girls were raring to go – until yours truly started. I had planned a handling session to beat all handling sessions, but unfortunately the little dears did not know what I was talking about, and gave me withering looks of incomprehension and pity.

My handling plan was clearly as much use as a chocolate teapot, and this was obvious after about two minutes – with fifty-eight to go! The only solution was to scrap the considered Plan A and somehow think of a Plan B very quickly. The answer was a very simple game of modified touch where you can pass in any direction. The rules were made up as we went along, and I suddenly saw the light: young players want to play games, and the coach can facilitate this desire and get the basics of the game across *if and when* the technical aspect is called for.

Hopefully the young players remembered the coaching advice that I tried to add to the little game with encouraging comments instead of the first aborted attempt at getting too complex a drill arranged – but it did teach me a valuable lesson. And I am fairly sure that many coaches of young players will empathize with this. We do enjoy drills and the coaching of specific skills with lots of detail and precision, possibly because such a session is relatively easy to set up and the elements that go wrong are generally predictable. But when do coaches concentrate on game understanding and players' flair and intuitive skills?

It is very easy to coach out flair and intuition, yet no coach will ever deliberately try to achieve such a negative result. However, many well-meaning coaches might never plan the sort of session that could develop these rich skills – because the type of session that may let them develop can go very badly wrong.

Unfortunately the package of drills is safe, predictable and manageable, and might, at first glance, seem to be doing a very well organized job. The session that is full of small games to develop understanding does not have the safety net of certainty and/or predictability – but when the coach develops the confidence to unleash his players into such sessions, they can benefit enormously. Such games will allow them to explore the possibilities and opportunities with a rugby ball, and they will become more quickly aware of the required skills and their own capabilities.

This book aims to offer advice on how and why, as well as offering drills and practices; it suggests that newcomers to the game might learn more from games for understanding than they ever will through a package of drills.

Some of it you probably follow anyway, but many 'coaches' out there are parents who are doing the job simply because their child is playing and there are no other coaches around to run the sessions. These volunteers deserve a medal, but it is vital that these same people have a basic understanding of the rudiments of the game alongside a sensible philosophy on what they are trying to achieve, and how they can best make a positive contribution.

If you have coached and/or you are a schoolteacher, you are used to organizing sessions and lessons for a high-spirited group who want action. But the tragedy is that more action can lead to more disruption and chaos if the exuberance is not managed – and that is perhaps why so many players, and children especially, learn through repetitive drills alone.

There are three distinct phases in the rugby coaching and playing cycle:

- The introduction of young beginners to the game, where there is no contact and the children are encouraged to play and learn through small team activities and games
- Tag rugby, where there is still no contact but the game starts to resemble the full game in attacking and defensive shape, the direction of the game and handling skills
- The game of rugby with contact in scrums, lineout, tackling, rucks, mauls and kicking

At all levels of coaching, *how* you get the message across is as important as the content of your sessions, and if a young player has a discouraging experience in the introduction to the game, he may not be around for the later stages.

So the coach of the early learners has a tremendous responsibility. If the introductory phases are fun and constructive, and if they give the children a sense of purpose and improvement, those young players will learn the basics of handling, controlling space, playing in a team, and how to score and defend within the rules that have been laid down. They will probably be encouraged to go on to the next phase and stick with the game.

There is little need for any formal coaching of skills in the early days, although a knowledge of the rudimentary basics of the game can help when planning what the activities and small games are meant to cover. It also helps if the coach understands those basics so that constructive advice, however basic, can be offered to the players.

Coaching Youth Rugby starts with coaching for beginners in mind in the early parts, develops into Tag Rugby, and then into coaching specific skills.

Positions (and Numbering) on the Pitch

15.	Full back (FB)	2.	Hooker (H)
14.	Right wing (RW)	3.	Tight head prop (TH)
13.	Centre (usually outside) (C)	4.	Lock (usually front jumper)
12.	Centre (usually inside) (C)	5.	Lock (usually middle jumper)
11.	Left wing (LW)	6.	Blindside flanker (BS)
10.	Fly half (FH)	7.	Openside flanker (OS)
9.	Scrum half (9)	8.	Number 8 (8)
1.	Loose-head prop (LH)		

CHAPTER 1

THE YOUTH RUGBY COACH

If you are the coach in charge of any group of young players you really do need to sit down with your colleagues well before you start. Some, perhaps all of you, may have no rugby background but are willing to help, because without you, the young people may not get to learn the game simply because nobody else can be found to run the sessions.

Do not let lack of rugby-playing experience put you off. There are various strategies that you can adopt so that you give the children meaningful exercise whilst they absorb the rudiments of a very complex game. Ask yourselves the straightforward question: 'Why are we taking on this coaching?'

There are many answers, but the children who will be learning the game ought to be at the top of this list. If the coach's ego initiates too many references to himself as coach, perhaps alarm bells should start ringing. Surely the object of the exercise will be to give a group of young people some meaningful physical exercise within forms or adaptations of rugby football.

If the players are total newcomers to the game, they will not need too much technical knowledge; being comfortable in handling the oddly shaped ball, learning catching and passing skills, and developing awareness of space, and how to create it, might be quite enough to aim for.

Nor will the coach require too much technical rugby knowledge, and might achieve these objectives with no more than some serious thought and inventiveness on how

to run small games. All he will need, once the games are planned before the session, is a rudimentary 'list' of skills that might be referred to once the game(s) starts.

If the subjects are already conversant with the rudiments of the game, their needs will differ slightly, but they need not be overloaded with technicalities. They may think they are ready for a 'proper' game of rugby because they have watched it live or on television, but the reality is that the whole game will be beyond them.

However, they will still be able to enjoy small-sided games where the rules can evolve and change each week; you do not have to play rugby on a proper pitch to develop many of the basic skills, but you will need to plan what you are going to do each session, and have a checklist of the basic shape of that session with rough times on each activity, plus a list of the equipment you will require, and a shortlist of the key points that you want to get across to your subjects.

Do not assume that you will remember everything that you covered, so a short written summary of the session will help greatly. You can also keep brief records of what worked and what didn't – and this information might help in the future.

A diary of your sessions and the key points on how they went could prove immensely valuable. It is certainly not a sign of weakness if you keep this brief record of what you did in each session, with a short analysis of what worked and what clearly did not. Do refer to this document, and always be on the lookout for what you see other coaches doing; if it seems to work it may be worth recording so that you can use it later.

What are Realistic Aims and Objectives?

You will probably overestimate what you might achieve in the early stages and before you ever start coaching the young players – you will merely be human if you dream of coaching future international players. However, the percentages are firmly against you in this, and you will, in all likelihood, be dealing with a cross-section of ability, ranging from pretty poor to quite good. Nevertheless the subjects are very young, and occasionally one or more might appear to be outstanding – but then again, it might be the most unlikely specimen who develops later in life, so do not be fooled by the superiority of the early physical developer. By all means extend the 'star' performer by asking a great deal of him, but never write off anyone.

If you can get your charges into an enjoyable, active environment where they can learn and develop handling (catching and passing), space awareness, evasion, how best to score, and how to get into some form of defence to fit in with the rules of the game you play, you will have done exceptionally well. Never assume that these seemingly elementary skills mean that your sessions will not be very good: when the basics are identified and practised and encouraged in small team games, a great deal will have been achieved. If, however, you start by aiming for too much advanced skill work, the ensuing result will probably be a failure. Start with realistic aims and expectations, and never be afraid to discuss the issue with other coaches who have been through the same thing.

If your young players learn to appreciate teamwork and how groups can work together in both attack and defence, you will have done very well. If you can enter the stratosphere and get your charges to appreciate that rugby is an ever-changing game where it is difficult to predict what is going to happen, you are flying; encourage these players to react to the constant change, and you will deserve a coaching medal.

The early introduction to rugby does not require the scissors, missmoves, dummies and sidesteps to be taught. If you run the right sort of game, these skills might appear quite naturally. However you, the coach, have to spot when somebody is naturally producing skill, and there is absolutely nothing wrong with bringing examples to the rest of the group's attention and running through the skill with a demonstration by the player(s) involved – or just by referring to it at a stoppage. Your players may take skill/s on board far more quickly if they see their peers produce it/them than they might if it is hammered home in a set of drills.

At whatever level you are coaching, do look out for the player who can score. There are many different body types in most teams, but a genuine try scorer will stick out immediately. He may not need as much assistance or encouragement as the rest, but he is a valuable commodity, and he will probably continue to be a scorer as he progresses in the game.

But a word of caution: although this player may well be far better than the rest, you do not want them to resent his skills if he starts to dominate. If you do have one player who is that good, try to encourage him to take satisfaction from making a break and playing another player into the game with a good pass. Let him be your playmaker, and do not be afraid to discuss with him why you do not want him to score all the time; there are other skills that he can improve, and you both know that he could have scored a hatful of tries if you had not encouraged him to make a hatful of scoring opportunities for the rest. However, he might need reassurance after every session that your 'pact' still exists and that you were aware throughout that he was doing exactly what you asked him to do when he was playing others into the game.

Your Role as a Coach of Young Players

Right from the start of your career in coaching young players, you need to determine why you are there and what your role is. The following is certainly not proscriptive, but it may offer a framework on which to build your coaching sessions.

You have to accept the responsibility for some or all of the following areas, which should be on any checklist of categories to improve through your plans.

- **Social development** using team games, skills that require cooperation between players, and encouraging a sense of fair play (right and wrong)
- **Mental development,** where young players improve in confidence and self-esteem, while appreciating that others may be very different in ability and performance
- **Physical development**, with plenty of healthy exercise and physical challenges
- **Skill development**, where *all* players improve their performance levels
- **Child welfare**

You also have to ensure that you give serious thought to your other responsibilities, which concern the following:

- Planning and running a safe, enjoyable and active session
- Understanding, even at a rudimentary level, what and how to coach within the activity or game
- Appreciating how game sense among young players will be best developed – and how to recognize it and comment on it when it is shown
- Having a knowledge of the rules of any game that you play
- Being able to referee that game competently and safely

Do plan each and every session so that you have contingency plans if something goes wrong. You will rarely get the precise numbers that you are expecting, so make sure that you have considered what to do with fewer players. At the head of your list and at the forefront of your planning should be a simple template that is used widely by RFU (Rugby Football Union) coaches, embodied in the acronym APES:

Active
Purposeful
Enjoyable
Safe

Communicating as a Coach

When coaching young players, it is as well to start off by acknowledging that, for example, you are physically vast and your voice is extremely loud; you may also use a piercing whistle to bring order to proceedings, and your young players will feel very small and threatened if you lose your temper and shout and/or whistle too stridently.

Try to think of coaching from *their* perspective, and start off by trying hard to modulate your voice. This is far from easy, and the decibels tend to rise as any session develops – but when you are constantly loud the players will end up by hearing your noise but without listening to what you are saying. And do you *really* need a whistle? Try running your session by voice alone: it is hard work, but it may prove to you that you do not need the blast of the whistle every time you want to announce something. Try to develop the skill of using the voice, whilst keeping the whistle as an aid in refereeing a game. By doing this, the whistle becomes very important and all activity stops when it is blown.

Then try to get down to the youngsters in a physical sense: instead of preaching downwards, why not kneel or crouch when you are offering advice or information? It does not take long, but you will be speaking to the players at *their* height level and you will not be regarded as some alien from the heavens.

When you are closer to their level, try hard to speak in a normal conversational tone. If you are excited, the message will probably be lost – especially if you are loud as well. Develop a habit among the group that there is absolute silence when the game stops for the coach to intervene, then you and any players who need to comment can do so in a way that allows the message to get across. If there is constant movement and chatter, you will never get the information to an individual or to the group.

There should never be an occasion when you swear, curse or blaspheme – apart from under your breath and so quietly that nobody hears it. You may be sorely tempted, but youngsters need positive examples. If you set the wrong tone it may be difficult later if you need to reprimand a player for something that you may have been guilty of on a previous occasion.

By the same token, the players must be guided from the first session (and for ever) in aspects of their behaviour: swearing, spitting, moaning about other players, cheating and not being able to accept refereeing decisions have to be taboo. You will have problems but you must not be afraid to be firm: lose this one and the game is not worth coaching anyway. Once you have started coaching young players, whether you like it or not, you are their mentor in more ways than just learning rugby: their behaviour is an important role that you have taken on. An acceptable code of behaviour from a noisy, lively group of children will not just happen because you announce once that this is what is required: you must be prepared to work hard at it, and never give up on what you demand.

This may sound too much like a schoolteacher, but you have to accept some form of moral responsibility when you take on these young players. They will require guidance on standards of kit, and you will have to be a good role model: for example, if you are untidy, they will have an automatic excuse to turn up in an untidy and dirty manner.

And start off by having a duty rota for pre-session and post-session. They need the responsibility of getting the equipment ready and then having it carried to the pitch – and they are learning valuable life skills when they have to count the balls at the end of the session and, if need be, go to look for any that are lost. These things will not simply happen, but you can make them part of your team's culture, and the players will be the better for it. It isn't all about playing rugby.

Coaches must agree that they will never be seen to disagree with any other coach, opponent, parent, supporter or referee. This may prove almost impossible under severe provocation, but you set the standards and you may have to bite your tongue more than once to restrain yourself. However, it has to be done and it must be part of your coaching charter.

Hopefully your players will be manageable,

and the basket will not have too many bad apples. But things will go wrong, however moderate, restrained, competent and organized you are, so why not have a set of club regulations – even if they are no more than guidelines? You do not need precise punishments for precise 'crimes' but it may help you to know that there is a procedure for dealing with difficult cases, which will hopefully be few and far between.

Most 'incidents' will be spur-of-the-moment things and can be dealt with without a committee meeting, but if you are faced with somebody who simply cannot accept the few disciplines of acceptable behaviour, that player has to know that there is a system to deal with him. A quick meeting between the culprit, yourself and another 'outside' coach may afford a bit of gravitas to the situation, and do not shirk from telling the player precisely *why* he is presenting problems. He may swear incessantly at home and/or spitting may be common – but both are frowned upon at the rugby sessions. He will not reform overnight so you probably need to try to accept gradual improvement as the way forward.

If a player really does keep on ruining the sessions for the other players, no system on earth will lead to reform and you need to get rid of him with an explanation of why you have had to take this step. Again, this will be best carried out by yourself and another coach, and you may need to explain to parents why you acted thus.

Luckily these incidents and tough cases will be rare, and your players will conform to sensible rules; if they cannot develop this part of their game, rugby is a poor choice of sport because they will find in later life that the referee has vast power, and an unwillingness to accept his interpretation of law will quickly result in early dismissal.

When you begin your coaching, early communication with your fellow coaches and players might save some difficult incidents later. If you and your colleagues have explained why there is a code of conduct and precisely what it is, the outcome may be far better than if you had explained nothing and simply dealt with misconduct as it occurred.

Once you start with a group, however young, you might consider bringing them in on what that group should demand on standards of behaviour. An agreement from them (however much you tweak it the way you wish) will have more force than simple announcements from coaches. So do spend a few minutes at regular intervals to get their thoughts on how certain aspects of their game and general behaviour have been going; it is all part of their development, and the majority will back you up in your aims if you give them the opportunity to speak.

At most stages of coaching and player development there will be parents around, and it is advisable to bring them in on what is acceptable behaviour as if they were part of the playing side. Some of them may not have a rugby background, and they may need to be reminded of the following code of behaviour:

- Everybody – players, coaches, parents – is there to enjoy the activity. Spectators and parents need to understand that all the young players deserve coaching and playing time
- Fair play is as important off the pitch as it is on the pitch
- The referee must have total support, especially from supporters. It will be totally confusing for a youngster if there is audible discontent/disagreement on decisions from the touch-line
- Encourage all players, and try to applaud the efforts of the opponents as well as those in your own side

Thank everybody involved at the end of the game, especially the referee and visiting players and coaches: without them there will be no game at all

Some of this may be difficult for a few parents, but it is a battle that has to be fought. One useful ploy is to have a spectators' charter, whereby parents have a useful role to play. Try to get them involved in helping, even if it is just being a water-carrier. The more they absorb the ethos of the game and its social aspects, the more likely they are to have a positive impact for good. Get them on board!

Providing for Players' Safety

The safety of your players must be of paramount importance. Already you will have undergone safety checks (the RFU Criminal Record Bureau (CRB) check, Regulation 21 (11–12)) to prove that you are not a threat to young people, so try to ensure that your coaching sessions are as rigorous in their planning for playing safety.

There will never be a foolproof and perfectly 'safe' sporting environment, but you can ensure that your sessions are as safe as is possible. This requires some thought and planning before the first session, and you should be aware at all times that you set the tone for what is safe practice.

- You will have playing rules for the games. Make sure that the players know them, and that they do their best to follow them. They will change as the game develops, but they are the rules at that stage
- All players must know your club's basic safety rules before they begin the first session

- Ask parents for information on any known medical complaint/problem their child has *before* you even start, and keep the information in a file for reference
- Always check the playing area/pitch and any equipment you will use before each session begins. This will take a little time but it is a habit worth getting into so that you are seen to be carrying out simple safety procedures
- All players need sensible footwear with the laces done up properly. If their boots have studs, check them before each session by simply rubbing your hand over both soles to check that there is no risk of bits sticking out and potentially causing injury
- All players should have their shirts tucked in. This offers less material to grab if defenders decide to hold on to something
- Jewellery must not be worn, as it can be very dangerous to the wearer if it catches on another player's clothing, and it can damage other players if it makes contact with their skin. If it cannot be removed, it may be possible to tape over it, but your players must try to help you with this one so that simple safety is ensured. One exception may be the use of goggles for U7–U12 players, 'who may wear specially designed and manufactured goggles provided that the child's optician certifies that (i) the goggles only allow that player to have properly corrected vision and do not substantially restrict any normal field of vision, and (ii) they do not constitute a physical danger to the wearer or other players' (RFU Regulation 15.7.5)
- The RFU recommends that young players should wear a gumshield (properly fitted from a dental mould) and shinpads
- If you use plastic poles for marking the pitch, do check that players carry them in

a safe way, because they may have a metal spike. The spike should point downwards towards the ground and the pole should never be thrown

- If you ever use tackle shields, insist that the holder uses both hands, one on each strap. Do not allow a one-handed carry across both straps, as this can lead to an arm injury on collision
- Pulling on a jersey (when there is no contact) should be banned
- Tag rugby has its own set of rules regarding how the tags are worn and what happens next
- Tripping must be banned from the outset and strictly refereed – and players must have the message reinforced whenever appropriate
- You must define what 'touch' means, and you must referee it. A heavy slap from a bigger player can put a younger, smaller person off the game
- Consider banning kicking any ball off the ground at any time. It will fly in strange directions and could easily hit an unsuspecting player
- Be aware at all times of size/weight imbalances in the work you are carrying out: the younger the players, the more pronounced will be the range of physical maturity
- You will need some basic first aid knowledge, and your club could well be the starting point for information. There should be first aid kit readily available, and an ice box full of ice cubes could be placed at the pitch side during all sessions. If ice is not available, ice packs that are activated with manual pressure might be useful, though these are a more expensive option than simple ice cubes

- If a player does have a heavy bump or sprain, the simplest and safest immediate treatment might be to follow that encapsulated in the acronym RICE: Rest, Ice, Compression and Elevation
- Your style of coaching may be the most influential aspect of injury prevention. Encourage 'heads-up' play at all times and you will automatically decrease the number of collisions and bumps. They will never be totally avoided, but you can minimize their occurrence while players learn a valuable rugby lesson
- Plan each and every session. This will greatly reduce the possibility of collisions when you know precisely which pitches/grids/channels you will be using, and how many will be in each one

The major consideration for all coaches at all levels of the game is that of player safety. There are sensible checks that should be made on a regular basis, and such things as gumshields and headguards ought to be looked at with younger players. Older players still need forms of checks, not least on their studs at training sessions. The referee checks footwear before games: try to get into the habit of doing this before practice.

During training, the coach will arrange areas of grids and/or channels. Ensure that there is *always a run-off area* at the ends and the sides so that players from different working areas cannot collide if they happen to come out of their working zone.

The safety of the players is largely in the coach's hands, so minimize any potential risk by being forever vigilant on what might go wrong. Always check the pitch, players' kit and the equipment you will be using: you can never be too careful.

CHAPTER 2

MAKING PRACTICES
FUN AND PRACTICAL

This chapter discusses small-team games and ball work to introduce young players to some of the principles of rugby while having fun.

You are ready to take your first session with a group of boys and girls of mixed size and physical ability. Some may know a bit about the game, others may know nothing: your task is to get them playing a game that is based on rugby while using a rugby ball. However, you must realize and accept that it is going to take a long time for these players to learn the full game of rugby, and the early activity will contain enough if there is lots of running with the ball in different types of rugby-related games.

Your introduction may be no more complex than giving each two players a ball and getting them to pass it one to the other anywhere within a marked area. At this stage you are simply trying to get them used to the ball's shape, and the first coaching point may be to pass and catch using both hands. Once they appreciate that this ball can behave oddly, you need to organize them into little games to get them running; too much 'chalk and talk' at this stage is not what they came for.

There are thousands of small-team games that have been invented and used by teachers and coaches all over the world, but this should not stop you from developing your own version(s), and there is no copyright to prevent you giving it/them your own name. You might even ask your young players to re-name an activity – even to come up with a game of their own that contains the key elements of what you are trying to achieve.

The ones who have seen rugby before will no doubt want to warm up because that is what adult players do. In fact they probably don't need this, and their normal activity at school and at play is unlikely ever to be preceded by a formal warm-up. However, you can be responsible for starting a habit that will be very useful as they progress in the sport. The main benefit at the early stages might be that it prepares the players mentally for the activity that is to come, it raises the heart rate quickly, prepares the body and muscles for the activity, and it may just help to prevent injury.

Whatever the game is, have a set of rules and encourage your players to play within those rules. A basic requirement must be to bring a sense of fun to the exercise while there is a maximum degree of activity and all-round involvement.

Do start with small numbers in teams, and increase those numbers only when the players' skills demand it. There is little point in having over-large sides, and excessive numbers are the main reason for the game breaking down. Ensure that you have plenty of balls available, and aim to use most of them whenever you can. Young players want to handle the ball!

Once all of this is covered, plan to ensure that there are not too many players in the

THE PITCH

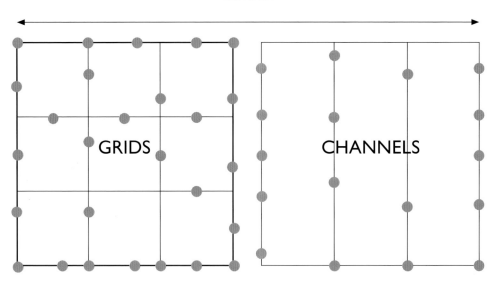

GRIDS

CHANNELS

Pitch, grids and channels.

same space. Only experience will assist you in getting it right, so arrange for just a few to be in a grid/working area until you get a better idea of what is safe.

The new coach may not be used to grids and channels, but they offer an area of work where he can be in control of many young players at the same time. And before your first planned session ever starts, set yourself a target of really attempting to increase the skills of all your players all the time, and spotting, then praising, good play. 'Good play' can mean many things to many people, but try your utmost to empathize with the less-able players, and understand that one good pass or an extra effort to get to a spot can be an enormous inspiration to such a player *if the coach recognizes it and comments on it.* Never forget your better players, but pay attention

to the youngsters who do not find the game easy, and let them know that you have spotted their success.

Feedback to any player is vitally important, but especially so to youngsters. Try to develop a degree of precision in what you say, because the more information you offer, the more the message will sink in. Rather than a vague, 'Well done' to a player, try to add specific praise, something like, 'Well done, you gave an excellent pass that was weighted nicely, and you have clearly learned from the last handling session'. It does not take much longer, but the recipient of the praise will know clearly what he has done correctly.

Then try to question youngsters. Ask for their opinion on why they think something went right or wrong. They will be stronger for attempting to analyse the game, and may well learn about skill more readily if they have some input on how it is being used. This is not to suggest that there is a free-for-all debate! Choose your moment, and work hard at developing players' comments as well as their rugby skills. It is not easy, so be prepared for answers that are not quite what you are looking for – and do have patience.

At all levels of coaching you must also be able to spot when something goes wrong, and try to put it right with advice or relevant practice. In the early stages of the game the errors will be fairly straightforward, and giving players an awareness of what is wrong may be enough at the level of small games. But as your coaching develops and players' skills improve, the coach will require a background of knowledge that allows identification of faults – and a repertoire of methods to try to rectify the problem.

In your planning, devise and use activities where errors are not that important. Even young players with limited rugby knowledge will know when they have dropped the ball, so they will not need a coaching report on such a fumble. When they are being introduced to the game, let them get on with playing, and don't stop the activity because of a dropped ball.

There are New Rules of Play (see Appendix) for Under 7, 8 and 9 players that have been introduced by the RFU to progress from 'Shaping the Game'. One of the principles behind the New Rules was to put the child first, and this is very important for all coaches. Instead of thinking about the full game of rugby then working that template down to age groups and beginners, try to start from the other end: offer exercise for all shapes and sizes that may one day lead to rugby. The exercise, team play and involvement should be enjoyable, and it ought to make all young players feel that they have achieved something in their activity. Mistakes are not at all important; far more important is a development of self-esteem among the youngsters, whatever their ability at the outset.

The Importance of Early Activities

Early activities are important to start the session, warm up the players, get them to concentrate on the activity, and introduce them to the basic skills of rugby.

This is a vital period of your session: if you do not capture the attention of the whole group now, it will become increasingly difficult to achieve it later. Get any session off with a bang, and ensure that the content is straightforward, manageable, and that there is some point to it.

Some elementary coaching points will be referred to that should be part of your coaching in these games and activities, but there will be further and more detailed coaching advice later in the book. At this stage you are simply trying to foster good habits, encourage exercise through various activities, and get across the rudimentary skills of rugby.

The games, practices and activities given here are a selection to suggest a range of what you can do in the early stages of introducing the game to youngsters. There are thousands of different activities, and many more variations on the themes.

Introductory/Warm-Up Activities

You are likely to be dealing with children who know little about rugby, and you have to grab their interest and enthusiasm from the first few seconds of the first session, and get them used to handling the ball. They will probably respond positively to little games that happen to be played with a rugby ball – and do not assume that there is anything wrong with these games if they have 'silly' names.

These little practices can be used at any time, particularly with absolute beginners who need to become comfortable with the odd shape and unpredictability of a rugby ball, whilst still having fun.

Individual Catching

Equipment: One ball per player. (If there are not enough balls, take turns and pass to a partner after a predetermined time or number of turns.)

Grid size: Keep a sensible space between players in case the ball is dropped and two players run to the same spot and collide.

Group numbers: One, if the number of balls allows.

Activity description:
(A) Throw the ball up and catch it.

Variations: Add a clap before catching. Throw the ball up and cradle it into the stomach. Add a clap before catching. Throw the ball up and catch it behind the back.

Skill development: Develop the catching so that only the hands are used for catching, then add a clap of both hands before the catch.

This can naturally develop into a competition to see who can make the most number of claps before the catch. Ensure that there is plenty of space between players as they will tend to throw increasingly high (to allow more claps), and they may have to move around more to get under the ball.

Activity description:
(B) Stand with the feet astride and pass

the ball around the body to bring it back to the starting point. Practise both ways. Bring in a competition to find out who can complete most passes (both ways) in a certain time.

(C) Stand with the feet astride. Hold the ball behind the legs, pop it up between the legs and catch it in front of the body. Repeat backwards. Bring in a competition to find out who can do most in a certain time – but stress that an attempt is not counted if the ball hits the ground at any time.

Back to Back

Equipment: One ball for each pair.

Group numbers: Pairs

Activity description: With a partner, stand back to back. Pass the ball side to side, making sure that both directions are used.

Variations: Pass the ball over the head and through the legs. Then work in fours, still back to back and standing in a square shoulder to shoulder. Pass the ball around the square.

Roll and Run

Equipment: One ball per group.

Grid size: About 10 × 10m

Group numbers: Six (but it could be any number) – five inside the grid and a runner on the outside.

Activity description: Player 'A' outside the grid rolls a ball into the grid, where the other players are waiting. He immediately runs around the grid and tries to get as far as possible before the fielders retrieve the ball and pass among themselves so that everybody handles.

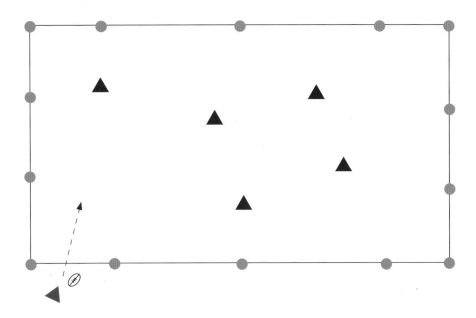

Roll and run.

Variations: Players in the grid have to touch the ball at a corner before passing, and it must not be the corner that was used immediately before the last pass. Each player has to perform a shoulder or forward roll before passing.

Touch

Equipment: Coloured bibs at the side of the touch area. Clear lines or coned playing space.

Grid size: This depends on numbers, but have a sensibly small area to start with, so that chaser(s) can gain some early success. Have another marked space next to the main area so that the pitch can be extended on the coach's command.

Group numbers: Four or five versus two in bibs.

Activity description: One or two chasers wear a bib. The rest of the bibs are placed off the playing area. The chasers touch (between the shoulders and the waist) those trying to evade the touch, and the winner is the last player who has not been touched.

Variations:
(i) As soon as a player is touched, he collects a bib and joins the chasing team, or

(ii) he kneels where he was touched and can then touch any runner who comes too close to him.

Interception (A)
Equipment: One ball per group.

Grid size: A triangular grid with three markers spaced so that players can pass comfortably within the area.

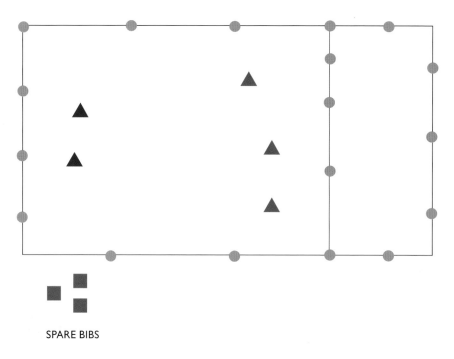

SPARE BIBS

Touch.

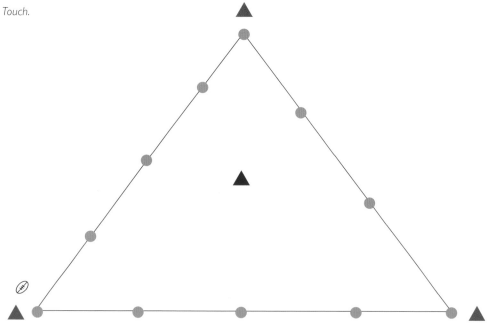

Interception (A).

Group numbers:
Fours.

Activity description: Assign three players to the three cones. The fourth player stands in the middle of the triangle and attempts to intercept the passes between the other three players.

Interception (B)
Grid size: This time the grid is square and must not be so big that players cannot pass the required distance.

Activity description: One player stands in the middle of the grid, and the other three stand on any three of the four corners. The player on the inside of the grid tries to intercept (as above in (A)) while the other three pass. However, no pass is allowed to be made diagonally, so one of the three must scan to

work out what is happening, then sprint to another corner.

No player can take a pass just after he has given a pass *if he is standing on the corner from which he has passed.*

Passing Relays
Equipment: Balls – enough for two per group; cones; poles, if there are enough available.

Grid size: 10m maximum to run forwards. Cones to mark channels 5m wide.

Group numbers: Between three and five (but there might be more if you are short of balls).

Activity description: Player 1 carries the ball and touches down at the cone next to the next runner – player 2. Player 2 picks up

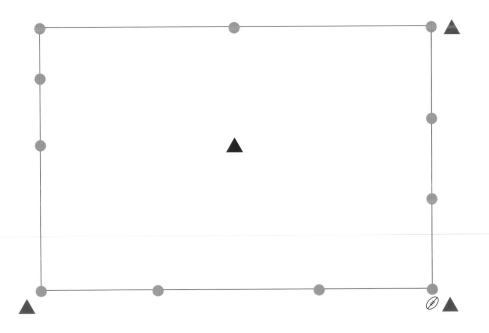

Interception (B).

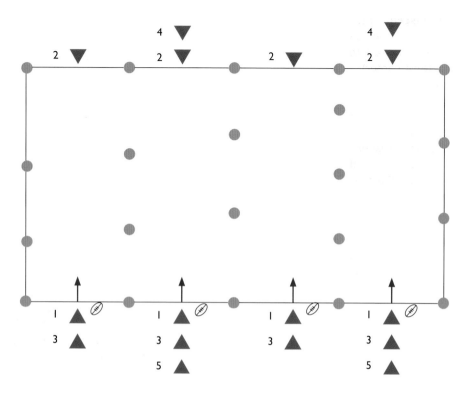

Passing relays.

and repeats at the other end of the grid – and so on.

The coach should stress (i) a touch-down, where the player is in control of the ball; and (ii) a lifting action and a two-handed lift when collecting.

An element of competition can easily be introduced by adding a stopwatch and finding out which team does the most carries in a certain time.

Variations: The ball is passed to a stationary receiver at the end of the run. The receiver is allowed to run on to the pass – but only after the ball carrier crosses a marker cone.

Poles are set up in a line in the middle of the grid, and the ball carrier has to swerve/weave while carrying the ball.

A roll (forward or side roll) can be added at any stage of each run. This can be at a marked spot or at a place that suits each player.

Robbery

Equipment: Four to six balls in the middle of the grid. Four cones to mark the corners of roughly a 20 × 20m grid. Enough cones to mark out the four treasure chests.

Group numbers: Three to six players on each corner.

Activity description: The purpose of the game is to 'steal' as many of the balls as possible, and get them back to each team's treasure chest (their corner).

The coach starts the game with a command, and the first player from each team tries to collect a ball and place it back in his team's treasure chest (which could be marked with cones in a circle shape). The ball should be placed with control into the chest.

He then tags the next player to go, and goes to the back of the queue. The new runner then attempts to retrieve a ball. Only one ball may be carried at a time.

When there are no balls in the middle, the designated runners (no others may join in) can steal from other teams' treasure chests.

The first team to get three balls back into their treasure chest is the winner.

There is to be no intervention to stop any 'robbery' of the balls.

Variations: The coach should have a couple of balls available to put into the middle if the game is going on too long.

Touch Ball

Equipment: Cones to mark the grid. One ball for each group of three. Bibs if two teams play against each other.

Grid size: 20 × 20m to start. This can be made smaller if the area is too big.

Group numbers: Teams of three. There should be no more than four groups in the grid at any time.

Activity description: One from each group of three is nominated as the runner. The other two must pass the ball to try to touch the runner while holding the ball, but they may not run with it. They must pass to get the ball close to the runner.

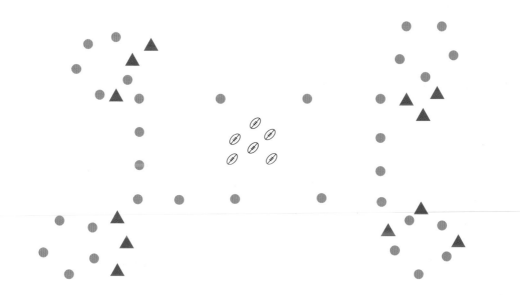

Robbery.

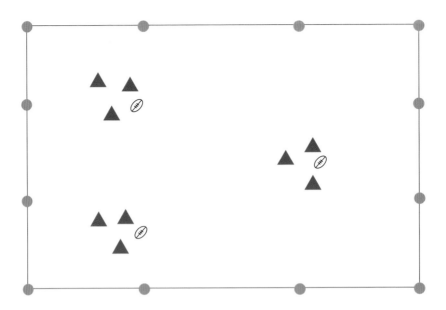

Touch ball.

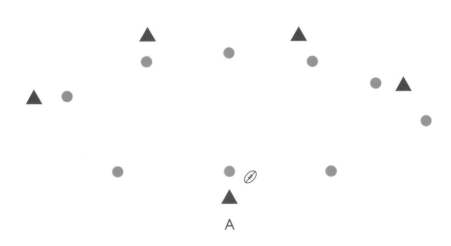

Semi-circle passing race.

Variations: If the escaping runner proves to be too quick for the passing skills, increase the team to four so that it becomes three versus one.

Form two teams (one to wear bibs) with a touching team and a running team. The rules are the same as above.

The game can be timed so that the winners are (i) the quickest to touch everybody, or (ii) the running team that can hold out longest before all are touched.

Semi-circle Passing Race

Equipment: One ball for each group.

Grid size: To suit the passing length of the group you are working with – and be aware of the player with the shortest pass.

Group numbers: Five to eight.

Activity description: Player A stands with the ball at the bottom of the semi-circle. The rest of the players fan out in a semi-circular shape facing player A. Player A passes to each of the other players in turn (and receives each player's pass in return).

As soon as player A receives the last pass of the sequence, he is replaced by the final passer and A moves to number 1 in the passing sequence while the other players shuffle across one place.

Variations: Play with two balls if the players' skill allows it, but do not allow the second ball to be passed too quickly or a logjam is a likely result.

Player A stays in that position for a set time and counts how many passes he makes.

Coaching points: This is a very good time to concentrate on the basics of an effective catching and passing technique for rugby

- Hold out both hands to receive a pass, and form the letter W by putting the thumbs almost together
- Passes should be aimed precisely at the target, the W shape
- The catcher must have total control of the ball before any pass is attempted. The pass must not be simply hurled to speed up the process.
- Watch for players favouring one side. If they do have a weak side, this is the time to identify it and try to improve the weaker side. One way to do this is to have a rule where passes have to alternate between left and right.

Triangular Drill

Equipment: Two balls for each group; cones to mark the triangles.

Grid size: The length of the triangle sides must suit the pass length within the group's range. Allowing a grid of 10 × 5m should give that space.

Group numbers: Five.

Activity description: Five players stand on the markers to form two triangles. The bottom centre player is part of both triangles. Two balls are passed along the lines of the triangles as shown by the dotted line arrows.

The competition/skill is to complete as many passing circuits as possible without dropping the ball.

Keep changing players' positions. This can happen after the ball is dropped, after a certain number of successful circuits, or after a certain time.

Variations: Pressure can be applied in a variety of ways:

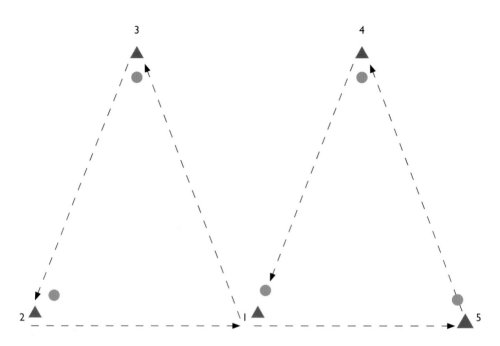

Triangular drill.

(i) Compete against another group(s) for a set number of circuits.

(ii) Add one more player to make one triangle into a square. This makes the players concentrate more as the regularity has been interfered with.

Coaching points: Once the competition begins, the players will make more mistakes and skill levels may deteriorate.

As two balls are in play, no player should pass to another if he is not ready for the pass, with his hands up in the W shape. Once a player does pass, he should immediately be ready for a pass from another player and should form the W.

Players should be encouraged to scan the whole grid so that they are all aware of where the balls are at any given time.

How Many Passes

Equipment: Enough balls to allow one to each pair.

Grid size: 20 × 20m to start, though this can be decreased (depending on numbers and skill levels).

Group numbers: Pairs. The number can be increased to threes when the players seem confident and ready.

Activity description: The aim is to make as many passes as possible without dropping the ball.

The player who has just passed must run five paces into space immediately after passing.

Variations: The activity can be timed –

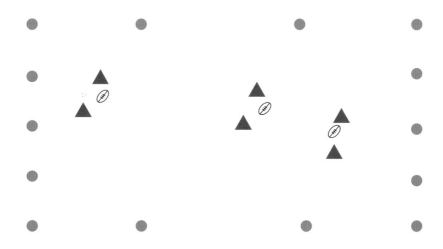

How many passes?

how many passes can be made in a certain time.

The coach can roam the grid, attempting an interception.

Extra 'defenders' can be added to attempt interceptions.

Coaching points: Collisions are possible. Keep stressing to players that they move into the biggest space available when passing or receiving, and remind them that they have to play with their heads up so that they can scan the whole playing area whilst looking for their partner.

Check that all players are moving throughout the practice.

You should also check that passes are given with both hands, and that the receiver offers the W target at all times.

Circle Passing

Equipment: Cones to mark the circle where each player will stand. Two balls per group.

Grid size: To suit the passing range of the players. Go smaller to begin with, and increase distances only when the players are not stretching to pass too far.

Group numbers: Five or six per group.

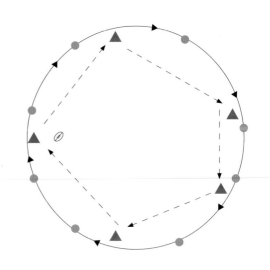

Circle passing.

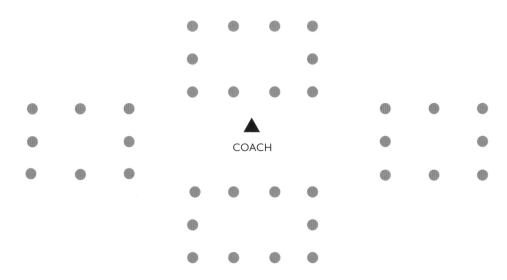

Coach at centre.

Activity description: The first player passes the ball, runs around the circle and tries to get back to his starting point before the ball and to take the final pass.

The second player repeats the practice, and so on. The direction of pass is changed frequently so that players do not just use their favourite passing side.

Variations: One group might compete against another; use a stopwatch to time the best effort.

Each runner must run around one stationary player in his circle before carrying on with his circuit.

In Summary

These games and activities are not by any means a full list, but they do offer a range that can cover most early skills in the game as long as the coach assists the players with advice and encouragement. The main elements of the early game are there, and the players will be handling the ball, looking for spaces, listen-

ing to instructions, scoring, competing sensibly and coming to terms with what a rugby ball feels like and how it is unpredictable in movement. You should also try to 'invent' your own games, even if it is merely an adaptation of an activity here, or one you have seen elsewhere.

Whatever the game, it is a good idea for the coach to carry a spare ball so that the activity can become almost seamless. The second ball can be introduced at any time and can be thrown to any player, so errors are largely unimportant as the game keeps moving and the players are always active. It is also a useful method of involving the less able player, as he can have possession as often as the coach decrees.

Delivery position for the coach can be important so that he sees as much as possible. At club level there will usually be other coaches and/or parents to assist. However, it could happen that a coach or schoolmaster is on his own and needs to see all. In this situation it is worth trying the formation where the coach is at the centre of all activity: it is a simple change of focus to go from facing three o'clock, then six, then nine and then twelve – and all activity can be maintained and supervised.

Learning to Fall and Roll

The skill of learning to fall and roll, and making contact with the ground painlessly, will come into the rugby equation at some time in all players' development, so any early work that gives confidence will be invaluable when contact is part of the game at a later stage. You will find there is a wide range of willingness/ability in most groups when they have to make contact with the ground: do not assume that it will be 'natural', and do try to 'lead' your players into the activity. Some players will leap into any situation, but there are others who may need more coaxing, encouragement and coaching.

If you do bring this activity into the sessions as a taster, maintain the FUN element: making ground contact must never be allowed to be

dreaded by some of the players. One way for the coach to get an idea of who is comfortable with ground contact is to play a game of 'Under the Legs'.

Under the Legs

Equipment: Cones to show where each player has to stand, with their legs astride.

Group numbers: Five or six per group.

Activity description: The players stand to the side of the cones and place their legs astride. On the coach's command, the front player runs to the back of the line and crawls through each player's legs. When he gets back to his original starting point and has both feet on the ground in the astride position, the player behind can go.

The circuit is over when the back player returns to his starting cone and has his legs astride.

Variations: Teams can race each other and/ or the stopwatch. They can start by forming a line with their hands on the shoulders of the

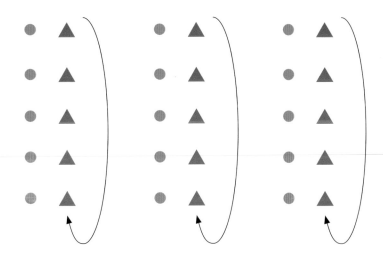

Under the legs.

31

player in front. The back player begins, goes under everybody's legs, and when he gets to the front and feels two hands on his shoulders, he calls the next player through. There needs to be a finishing line for this variation.

Coaching points: Keep reminding the players of the rules. Once the competition starts the feet will come off the ground, and there will be hands that are not on the shoulders of the player in front.

Rolling

This last exercise can develop naturally into rolling. If this is done badly, youngsters may remember the experience and be reluctant to try it later. Most, however, will be perfectly happy with the skill, so be ever alert for the child who is clearly struggling.

Also do not assume that everybody will have done this at school. Some will require no instruction, while others might need real time and effort to perfect the techniques of *any* form of rolling. You might run a special session at some stage just for the ones who do not perfect the technique – an early start to your usual practice time would offer them the chance to improve.

Shoulder Rolling

The shoulder roll is simpler than a forward roll and probably has more direct relevance to rugby; it is a skill that can be taught even to those who do not relish it.

The following is for a right shoulder roll; the procedure is reversed for the left:

- Crouch forward (when stationary) with the weight over the right bent knee and the back rounded
- Tuck the chin into the chest and dip forwards so that you can look backwards through the legs
- Keep bending the legs whilst moving

slightly forwards to place the back of the right hand, then the right forearm, on the ground
- The weight keeps moving forwards to initiate a roll on to the back of the right shoulder
- Keep rolling into a standing position with both hands up and ready for a pass

Variations: A ball can be passed by a partner just as the roller moves into the crouch position, with hands showing the W position.

The crouching start can be replaced with a standing start (which automatically moves through the crouch start).

The player, when confident and comfortable with the skill, can jog into the roll. Other variations would be to produce the movements while holding a ball; to pick up a ball from the ground just as the back of the hand goes to the ground; or to put the skill into loop relays.

Coaching points: Keep the speed down – it is a jog, not a sprint, and be prepared to assist/support those who need help.

This skill is very useful when a player has been ankle-tapped, knocked off balance, or has simply fallen over when in possession of the ball.

Stress the importance of controlling the ball during a roll, and/or getting up to be fully ready to receive a pass.

This work is to give young players confidence when they have to come into contact with the ground, so the coach must ensure that confidence in what they are doing is of utmost priority. Always *go back a stage* if players are not coming to terms with what is required.

Early Contact Experiences

Learning how to make contact safely can be worked on well before young players start specific rugby contact with each other, and could follow the work that has been done on rolling.

Early conditioning might start with contact between the player and the ground with a variety of forward, side and shoulder rolls, as were covered earlier. Once the players are confident with these basic manoeuvres, they can perform them while holding a ball.

As in all other activities, these contact experiences require careful monitoring, and the rules must be stressed so that the activity does not degenerate into fighting.

- Two hold hands and each tries to pull the other over a line (or cone)
- One lies on the ground and resists his partner's efforts to roll him over
- One goes on to his hands and knees and resists his partner's efforts to roll him over and off balance

Contact does not need more than an introduction in the early stages, and variations of small-sided games and tag games will provide the bulk of what is being done. Therefore introduce rolling and contact, but do not make it the most important element in the game.

Developing Handling Skills

In the development of handling skills it is not necessary to rush the process of achieving backward passes, and much early work will need to be spent on the following:

- Giving and taking a pass
- The awareness of spaces, even on very small pitches
- Team work
- Defending within the rules
- Scoring within the rules

Children really enjoy discovery and inven-

tion while having fun through games; if you can stimulate your charges in the environment that you create, they will respond with enthusiasm and effort. Conversely, if you are responsible for their boredom, do not expect too much from them.

Rugby Netball

At some stage the players will have grasped some of the game's basics through your activities, and you may feel that they are ready to move into a game that resembles the full game more closely. Do not rush this process, but the version known as rugby netball is simple, easily controlled and run, and can be constantly amended to suit the coach's and the players' needs.

Start with as few rules as possible, and add new rules when the players seem to have mastered the current restrictions. A sensible idea is to ask the players themselves about how the developing game's rules can be adapted or changed, and they will come up with some interesting answers; if they don't, the good coach will massage and manipulate their answers so that he ends up with what he wanted in the first place and what they *thought* they had said.

The pitch can be marked quickly and easily with cones or poles: the precise measurements are unimportant, just make the size of the pitch appropriate to what is required for the number of players, and to what you hope to achieve.

At this point it may be advisable to offer a word of warning as to the over-use of cones. They are easy to use and very simple to carry, but young players in particular may be better served in many cases with poles as markers. With cones the players have to look down to see where they are or where they have to run, yet we need to encourage a 'heads up' approach, and poles will probably assist more in that conditioning: young players might just get used to looking ahead for longer periods, rather than looking down for the ubiquitous cone(s).

Do not be afraid to keep changing the pitch size; an increase in the dimensions will make attack easier, and a decrease ought to have the opposite effect. And at all times, keep the numbers as small as possible so that all players have an opportunity to handle the ball and participate in the game.

Rugby netball is simple to set up, it puts a premium on scanning and using space, and the rules can be changed at any time. It is an activity that can be used as a template for all age groups and abilities.

The first game can be organized according to very simple rules:

- The players may pass in any direction within the pitch
- Defenders cannot make any contact, but they can intercept a pass
- No player may run with the ball

- A point is scored for each successful pass (or the sequence of passes can be timed, so that the team that keeps possession for the longest period wins)
- The sequence ends when the ball is dropped or it is intercepted

In the next game the rules might allow a certain progression:

- The ball carrier can run with the ball but must pass when touched below the shoulders. The same scoring system as in the first game is used
- Alternatively the ball carrier may run with the ball and the defenders can only intercept passes. To stop one player simply keeping possession, the aim might be to see how many passes can be made in a certain time

This can then progress to a game where you score by getting the ball to your 'goalkeeper'.

The game of rugby netball is also simple, in

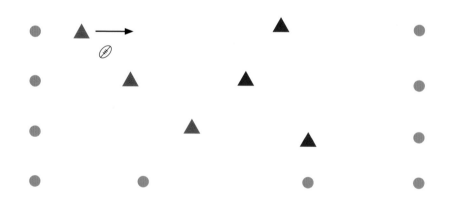

Rugby netball.

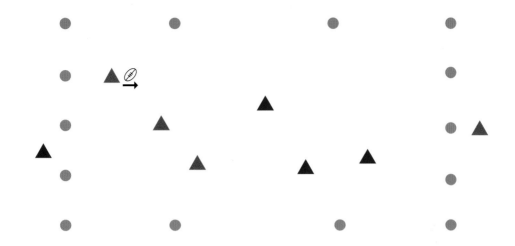

Rugby netball with 'goalkeeper'.

that the red team has to get the ball to the red 'goalkeeper' to score, and the blue team has to hit the blue 'goalkeeper'. Start off with rules that allow free movement, but with the following restrictions:

- The 'goalkeeper' can move sideways but not forwards on to the playing area
- There is no contact: the defenders try to intercept a pass
- The team in possession can run and pass as they wish in any direction, but any player who is touched by an opponent must pass (you can add a rule that suits you such as 'within two more paces' or 'within a second') to another player, but he may not score with that pass
- If the attacking team drops the ball, the opposition gets possession
- Interceptions are allowed
- When there is a score, the 'goalkeeper' is replaced by another player so that all players take their turn at different positions. At each score, you might move all players in the middle to the wing positions so that

nobody becomes too settled in their area of competence

There is a great deal of coaching that can be offered in such a game, but encouragement and praise are vital. At this stage, you really can start to coach rugby skills without seeming to do so – and you certainly do not need years of rugby experience.

Throughout this game (and in many others) you might encourage the following skills:

- That at all times, the player with the ball and all support players try to get into space
- To pass so that the receiver has to run on to the pass and is not static
- That decoy/support players work hard even when they may not receive the pass
- Two-handed passing and receiving
- Sympathetic passing, where the ball is not hurled at the intended receiver
- Constant scanning (heads up) from all players to see what is unfolding and developing in front of them

Try to encourage and develop the *hard-work ethic of various support runners* getting into space to allow the opportunity of more than one place to pass for the ball carrier. This will not happen naturally with too many players, so you need to encourage selfless running into space by players who do not have the ball. When this is achieved, life gets very difficult for defenders, and this 'truth' transfers into the highest levels of the game. Once young players understand this, the game can become much simplified in their minds. If various support players get into a space, the defence will struggle to cope.

As the players start to move freely and begin to understand the game, introduce different rules, such as the following:

- Passes have to be given with *both hands on the ball*
- The catcher must show that he is trying initially to *catch with both hands* – unless the pass is wide of the intended target

- Encourage support runners to show *both hands as a target all the time*, and try to get them to show the letter W with their hands
- If the defenders simply stand back and guard the 'goalkeeper', cone off an area in which no defender may stand unless he is running across it
- The attacking team must give a backward pass to start their handling
- This can develop into two passes backwards before attacking forwards (though the defence will probably have to be restricted, as two backward passes will be nearly impossible if the defenders are allowed to roam wherever they like)
- The coaching element can be constant, and support attackers should be encouraged to *'lose' a defender* with change of direction, pace and line of running. These are vital aspects of the 'real' game, but this mini version allows far more opportunities to practise *deception and evasion*
- Do ask the players themselves to suggest

'W' hands – shape for taking the pass.

changes in the rules to make the game more interesting and more challenging. Make sure the changes are achievable, however, and do not let them become over-complicated so that the fun element disappears with those changes.

This game can easily become a template on which to introduce young players to rugby. There will be variations, and the thoughtful coach will keep on adding to the ways in which the rules offer the players a challenging and enjoyable game environment. However, the process must not be rushed, or progress will definitely be slowed. Get to the point where an enjoyable, competitive game can be enjoyed that is within the scope of the players' skills. There is absolutely no need to get to the next coaching point or development stage: let the players' enthusiasm and success be the guide. Do not confuse them by 'advancing' when they are not ready for the jump.

Even at this early stage of development, encourage *decoy running*. Try to get your players to understand that a dummy runner may

have a profound effect on what the defenders see and the players may just pick up a vital skill at an early stage.

Developments in Rugby Netball

The coach should carry a spare ball so that any form of the game can be kept moving and stoppages are virtually eliminated. Just introduce the new ball to suit the game and the players.

Once the players have got used to the game and they begin to understand that errors are not the most important part of the agenda, there are ways to make it more rugby specific:

* A restart or turnover might start with two passes backwards, which could develop into…
* …those two passes having to be made to players who are running forwards…
* …which can soon become three passes (and the game emerges)

However, these developments in the game will not be necessary or appropriate for some

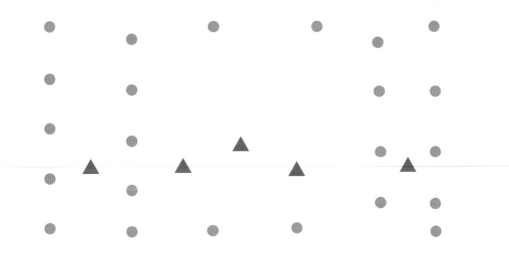

Avoiding the honeypot.

time. Ensure that the young players are fully capable at any stage you reach, and do not introduce 'extras' that may be beyond the group's skill levels.

As in all coaching games, the defenders will usually dominate as attackers learn new skills. Nevertheless it is very important to condition the role of the defenders (and numbers) so that the attackers have a good chance of success. Constant failure with a new skill will do no good, so the coach must ensure that the progression is not happening too quickly and that the attack can succeed.

You may already have come across the 'honeypot' syndrome where the players are all attracted to where the ball is. One method of controlling this is to mark out two areas up the sides of the pitch, and to allocate two attackers to stay within those bounds – but remember to keep changing them after a score. You might also have a rule where one of the side players has to handle the ball before a score can be made, which will make the other members of the team aware that there is width to the attack.

But the coach having that extra ball can be invaluable, as it can be played to the widest player, and width will be achieved with a single pass from the coach when he introduces a new match ball each time.

A variation of this game can be used later right through the age groups. It can be a game in itself for younger players, or a warm-up and preparation for older ones. The rules can be altered at any time to suit the coach's requirements, and full activity is maintained throughout.

Coaches are inclined to teach in the way that they learned, so try to be aware that players have vastly different learning styles. Some may not get the coaching message from just one method of getting the point across, and they may not want to admit that in front of their peers. Try to create an environment with as much activity as possible, as this ensures that all players will have a decent chance of learning the basic coaching message.

In these early learning stages it is vital that the process is not rushed. If the skills demanded are beyond your players, it is not a sign of failure if you go back a stage and simplify things. You will have a lot to do in achieving even the following skills:

- Giving and taking a pass
- Awareness of space, even on very small pitches
- Teamwork
- Defending within the rules
- Scoring within the rules

At some stage in this introductory phase where young players are probably handling a rugby ball for the first time, you may decide to introduce elements of skill coaching. You will probably not want to go beyond running forwards while passing the ball, but this is never simple. However, there are handling practices later in the book, which can be used or conditioned to suit your needs.

Rugby netball can offer a very simple game for all ages and levels of ability. It can be played right through the coaching process, and young players should find it a useful introduction to Tag Rugby.

CHAPTER 3

TAG RUGBY

This section on Tag Rugby has three main objectives: to show coaches what comes next after players' earliest introduction to rugby; to give the Tag Rugby coach, who may well have been coaching beginners up to this point, a synopsis of what Tag is all about; and to suggest some games and activities to introduce youngsters to Tag.

The skills, with the exception of contact skills, are the same as are required in the full game, and many of the practices shown after the Tag Rugby section can be utilized by the Tag coach.

The game itself is relatively simple to set up, and with encouragement from the coach, the players should absorb the main points that are important in running forwards and passing laterally. Never, however, underestimate how complex it is for some young players to achieve forward momentum while passing sideways, and it may require serious coaching time and effort for the players to take it on board.

Then there is the constant problem of players in possession running blindly until they are tagged, without very much thought of support players who might offer more if the ball were passed to them. This tends to get worse as soon as competition is introduced.

The coach must encourage handling and passing before the tag takes place if support runners are available, but this seemingly simple development will often prove to be difficult, as young players tend to forget or disregard the rest of the team once they get the ball in their hands. All the coaching advice may be forgotten when a player receives the ball and wants to run – so be sympathetic.

The game is a stepping stone towards having confidence in finding space, passing to another player in a better space, and exploring different ways that space can be utilized. There are many opportunities for all players to handle, but do not worry about errors such as a bad pass or a dropped ball – rather, treat such things as part of the learning process, and whenever possible, just play on and deal with the next bit of play. There is enough whistling for errors later in the players' rugby education and experience.

It is quite possible that you will have a new set of players from the ones you coached in the introductory phases for beginners; it all depends on how your club sets up the coaching arrangements, and who does what. However, if you are keen to follow a group of young players right through their coaching experience, do think twice about this: their playing skills will, in all probability, develop faster than your coaching, and it could well be that your benefit to the coaching system is with a certain age group.

There is a two-year window for Tag (U7s and U8s) before contact comes into the game. In your period in charge you will have done exceptionally well if you can get the players in your group to learn the following skills:

- Recognize scoring opportunities, and how they are made possible and more likely with handling skills
- Recognize how an organized defence within the rules can make scoring more difficult for the attack
- Learn how to use handling skills and game sense to score
- Learn and understand how a pass, and how it is given, can beat a defender
- Appreciate how the team is defending, and fit in with that

Tag is a simple, safe game that can be played as a game in its own right or as an activity that is part of the progression to rugby proper. Its key elements are enjoyment, with plenty of running and handling. The game keeps changing from attack to defence, and youngsters soon start to appreciate the ever-changing nature of the game and the steps they need to take to deal with those changes in the middle of a quick game.

While individual flair and skills can be shown, there is still much opportunity for teamwork, cooperation, collective responsibility and communication.

Equipment and Rules

To play Tag the following equipment will be required:

- One pair of tags for each player + a velcro belt for attachment
- One ball for each player (if possible) for the introductory and warm-up stages
- Cones
- Bibs
- A first aid kit that has been checked regularly so that any used items are replaced. (A sensible club rule might be that the person who uses any item from

the kit is responsible for replacing it or informing the club if a replacement is required)

The tags are attached and worn in the following way: the belt goes around the waist and the two tags are attached by Velcro, with one tag hanging down on each side. The belt must be worn outside all other clothing and must never be covered, so that belt and tags are visible and unobstructed at all times. There should be no part of the belt hanging loose and flapping. Any spare part of the belt must be tucked in under the main belt.

The rules of Tag are as follows:

- A player is tagged when an opponent (defender) takes one tag
- When the ball carrier is tagged, neither that ball carrier nor the tagger can re-join the game until the ball is passed *and* the tag is returned and reattached. (This is an important element of discipline for both players and must be refereed strictly as the players will want to get back into the game as quickly as possible. It immediately frees up more space for the rest, and the procedure is starting to resemble contact rugby where the tackler and the tackled are out of the game for a short time)
- When a player is tagged, he may pass within three steps or he may stop and pass within three seconds
- The ball carrier may dodge potential taggers with evasive skills, but…
- …*may not* use hands or the ball to fend off a would-be tagger, or attempt to guard or shield the tags in any way
- The tagger may not pull the ball from the carrier's grasp
- There is to be no contact at any time. If it occurs, the game must be stopped

immediately, the offender spoken to, and perhaps an explanation given so that all players understand the rules
- The penalty for contact is a free pass to the non-offending team

The object of the game of Tag is to score tries with downward pressure on the ball beyond the opponents' goal line. There are, however, some safety requirements that have to be taught to the players:

- The pressure on the ball must be downwards and over the goal line
- There must be no diving to score: all players must be on their feet at all times
- If a player scores when on his knees, the score is allowed to stand. However, at the natural stoppage for the try, the players must be reminded that they are to be on their feet
- No player may attempt to stop the grounding of the ball at any time or by any means
- After a try, the game restarts with a free pass from the centre for the non-scoring team

There is little point in going straight into a full game of Tag unless you are with a very gifted group of youngsters, but even a high-flying group will benefit from starting with an introductory period when you build up the skills and rules of the game so that the players can cope with the later full game. These small-sided games can be an effective warm-up/preparation period, and they will allow maximum opportunity to run, get the ball in hand, and develop evasion skills.

In all early learning days in rugby, time and space (or lack of both) can make improvement difficult. You have to make sure that the attackers have the opportunity to gain success or they will soon learn that handling the ball equates to failure; you want them to see success as the likely outcome.

Small-sided and modified games are an integral part of a game-centred approach to coaching rugby. This process requires the coach to select appropriate activities that allow the players to experiment and to work out solutions for themselves so that they do not rely on being told what to do by the coach. If a mistake is being made and repeated, the situation can be reconstructed and the player(s) can be asked how best to put things right. Questioning is a key part to allowing the young players to work out solutions.

Sometimes players will recognize what the problem is, but will not have the technical skills to put it right immediately. However, the technical deficiencies in the early stages will not stop them from enjoying appropriately selected games. Active participation will maintain interest and enthusiasm, and the technical aspects of the skills of the game can be worked on at a later stage.

Use grids for these small-sided games, and experiment with the size of the pitch. There is no 'proper' grid size, and experience will allow you to get the pitch dimensions pretty much right.

Small-Sided Introductory/ Warm-Up Tag Games

There are countless small-sided games in a small area that can be adapted for the introduction of Tag; four of these are described below.

Three versus Three
This Tag game is manageable and allows the players plenty of opportunities to experiment with attack and defence. Use the rules of the

full game, but the defenders must retreat 5m after each tag if the ball carrier stops to pass. This has a dual purpose in that space is made available for the attack, and the defenders are learning to stick to the rules by being disciplined, which is part of the defensive learning curve.

Seven Attackers versus One Defender

As soon as any player is tagged and passes the ball, he removes his tags and joins the defence. This can be turned into a small-scale competition to find out who manages to evade the taggers and ends up as the sole ball carrier most times.

British Bulldog

This is a Tag variation on the old game. The rules are as follows:

- The pitch should be 30m wide and 40m long
- There are five or six players with tags, and one ball each on one goal line
- One tagger defends as the whole group of attackers runs through the grid, and all attempt to score at the other end

- When a player is tagged, he joins the defending player(s)
- The winner is the last remaining ball carrier who has not been tagged

There are three developments that can be made on this particular Tag variation:

- When the defenders have tagged two ball carriers, let the remaining attackers play with just one ball, and run and pass in any direction to attempt to score a try. The aim is to score without running out of attackers – although they do not join the defence when tagged, but play on with the tagger and the tagged player, waiting until the belt has been replaced
- As above, but the pass from the first tag must be passed backwards. Then the players may run and pass in any direction
- As above, but the first two passes must be passed backwards

Stick in the Mud

The rules for this Tag variation are as follows:

- The pitch should be 30m wide and 40m long

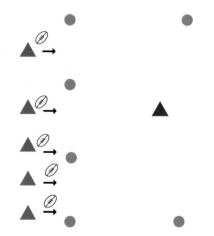

British bulldog.

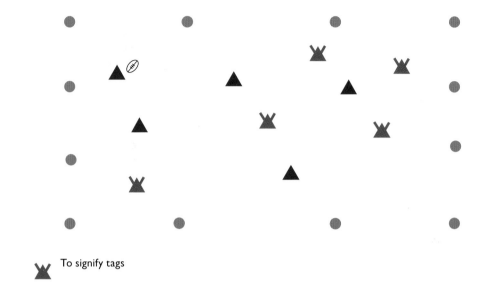

 To signify tags

Stick in the mud.

- Teams should be of three, four or five, and team players should wear bibs when in the grid
- The opponents, wearing tags, run around the grid trying to evade tagging
- When a player is tagged, the tagger returns the tag and both stand still in the grid with both hands above their head
- Both are free to re-enter the game when one or other of them is touched with a ball by another player
- Another variation is that they are free to re-enter the game when another ball carrier crawls through the legs of one of the pair (who should stand with legs astride)

Tactics will begin to emerge, and the aim should be to get all passes going backwards after the introductory games. This may need sympathetic coaching, as it is far from simple to run forwards and pass back – but there are many practices that will assist players in achieving this end.

One of the coach's hardest tasks will be to get the players to pass when running with the ball, so a 'local' rule may be needed – something along the lines of five strides maximum before passing for all players in attack. This may encourage a 'heads up' approach, as they will have to look for support runners instead of simply running with the ball until a tag occurs.

The essentials of the full game can be encouraged at this stage: these can be itemized as follows:

- To go forwards
- To carry the ball in two hands
- To stay on your feet
- To aim for a space(s), or to pass to another player to put him into a space

The Full Game of Tag

The aim of Tag: To score tries and prevent the opposition from scoring by adhering to the rules of the game (see above).

The teams: Consist of five to eight players on the pitch, plus substitutes who can be used at any time (these are known as 'rolling substitutes'). Mixed gender sides should be encouraged.

The technical aspects: The maximum dimensions of the pitch are 60 × 30m, with a 5m in-goal area at each end for scoring.

The ball size for U7s and U8s is a 3, and for all other ages up to and including U14 is a 4.

The wearing of custom-made mouthguards (made from a dental impression) and shinguards is recommended by the RFU.

The duration of games: In a festival, U7s and U8s should not participate for longer than 50min. U9s and U11s are restricted to a maximum of 70min. If a game becomes too one-sided (with a difference in scoring of six or more tries), that match should be shortened.

Passing: The ball must be passed sideways or backwards, and there may be no handing on (the ball must leave the passer's hands) instead of a pass.

If the ball is handed on, or is passed or knocked forwards, a free pass is awarded to the non-offending team *unless there is a clear advantage to the non-offending side.*

Free passes: Each half starts from the centre of the pitch with a free pass.

A free pass is awarded from the side from where the ball goes out of play, and from where the referee makes a mark on the field of play where an infringement takes place.

At a free pass the following rules must be observed:

- The opponents must be 7m back from the mark
- The receiver of the pass must be stationary and within 2m of the pass, but he may

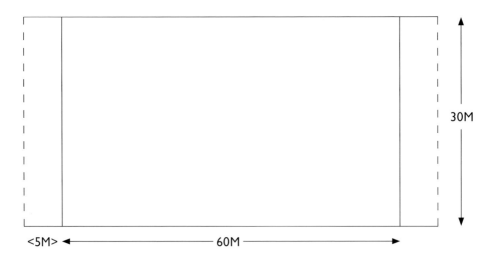

<5M> ◄——————————————— 60M ———————————————►

30M

Tag pitch dimensions (maximum).

start to move forwards before the ball leaves the passer's hands to receive the ball while moving forwards

- The player with the ball must hold it in both hands and must play it when the referee calls 'Play'. The pass must go backwards to a player on his team. No player may run until the pass is made
- If an infringement takes place, or the ball goes into touch, over the goal line or within 7m of the goal line, a free pass is awarded to the non-offending team 7m from the goal line

There is a full list of all Tag rules and regulations on the RFU coaching website www.rfuca.com – also coaches can get more detailed information concerning offside, obstruction, ball on the ground and children's welfare.

There will come a time when the coaching of basic skills becomes necessary. Once Tag Rugby starts, the coach will need to isolate some of the components if the game breaks down because they are not being well performed.

There is no contact in Tag Rugby so handling skills, evasion and defending within the rules are at the core of the game. Many handling skills will develop naturally in the right environment, and Tag certainly makes the youngsters aware of how best to score. Taking the tags also forces them, without their knowing it, into something approaching preparation for a tackle, as they have to reach towards the opponent's tags to try to get them.

The skills and practices in the following chapter may be necessary at some stage(s) in the development of Tag Rugby.

CHAPTER 4

COACHING AFTER TAG RUGBY

This chapter investigates teaching and shaping the fundamental skills for players of all ages and ability. The early age groups will have just moved up from Tag Rugby, and that can still remain an ideal game on which to base your coaching. It will continue to offer a medium where handling, passing, running and evasion are at the core of activity.

There is a belief among players and coaches alike that rugby coaching somehow changes dramatically as players become older. Obviously the contact elements of the game change, but the core principles remain and are too often overlooked in the coaching of older players. Most would accept that there ought to be a *fun* element for younger players, but why should that suddenly alter as a player gets older? Teams and players in the community game will probably develop more dramatically if they actually enjoy the practice sessions, so do not assume that fun ceases to exist at a certain age. Keep the *fun* element in your coaching of all age groups and adults.

The same goes for playing small-sided games. The coaches of younger players generally agree that the game's intricacies can be best learned in games. Yet when players develop into adults we tend to forget that they enjoy playing – even at training sessions. The coach should encourage playing small-sided games whenever possible, however old (or young) the players are. They will generally work harder in such a game than they might in a drill which can be practised for so long that

boredom sets in. Such games can also provide a fitness element that is probably far more productive than running around the pitch.

There are variations that the inventive coach can use, when players of all ages and abilities work hard in a competitive environment, where handling and evasion are the key to success. The coach can also keep on stressing that rugby is ever-changing, and that they, the players, must practise ways of finding solutions to those changes. Drills have a purpose, but problem solving is probably best achieved in a game that the coach has set up.

These conditioned games can eventually lead to ones with live tackling. This will need to be monitored closely, and rules on how and where a tackle may be made will have to be stressed. Tackle suits are ideal for this type of game, but even if your club does not have any, there still needs to be a set of rules that first insist on players tackling no higher than around the hips, and secondly, that ban confrontational tackles from the front.

Once you start your coaching sessions with conditioned games, it might be worth thinking of the *whole-part-whole* theory, which has been useful to coaches for many years but has never become old fashioned:

- If the players are comfortable with what they are doing and can cope with what is asked and required, leave well alone and keep with the whole game or skill

- If a stumbling block emerges that is interfering with progress, take a short time to look at the *part* (for example, a certain skill to be improved), but…
- …get back to the *whole* as soon as you can

Remember, however, that you must learn to recognize and acknowledge skill, effort, endeavour and improvement within the small-team game. The player who is absolutely breathless after playing a supporting role as you asked him, will hardly keep on doing it if he feels that nobody is watching – so encourage him with positive feedback and praise. And do remember that it is unusual for a player of any age or ability to make an intentional mistake.

Little bits of advice to individuals as the game goes on may produce results and improvement, but rein yourself in when you start to get too technical. Players may be better equipped than you give them credit for, when it is a question of working out what succeeds and what their capabilities are: the good coach will almost let them coach themselves until a wise word of advice is needed.

Whenever teams or groups are selected, make sure that you work hard to avoid cliques building up. All players will want to be with the people they know – or with the better players – and this does not alter as the players get older. Your job is to develop team play, not a team within a team.

Whichever version of rugby you come up with, experiment with pitch size to stop the players from operating in their own comfort zone. This might ensure that the better players do not become bored because the game is (or seems) too easy.

The appropriate ball size and its condition is a vital requirement, as young players in particular need to be able to handle the ball: you will need a size 3 for U7s, U8s and U9s; size 4 for U10s, U11s, U12s and U13–14s; and size 5 for U15 – U18s and adults. Do check also how well it is inflated, as too much pressure will make handling skills more difficult. A ball with a bit of 'give' in it will be relatively easier to catch than one that is over-inflated – and never be afraid to adjust the size of the ball you are using, and/or to check how hard it is inflated to suit what you need for the players you have.

One of the biggest problems at senior club level is the condition of the balls used at training sessions. If handling is to be at the centre of activity, a decent ball that has been inflated correctly and cleaned is surely a vital requirement. Yet few coaches seem bothered enough about this. Try to ensure that the players have a ball that looks and feels right – and develop a system where the players are responsible for getting all the balls back to the kit room at the end of each session.

The Shape of a Session

All sessions need a shape. However, never be afraid to keep things simple: over-elaboration and complexity do not equate to successful and meaningful exercise.

The best sort of introductory exercise is to go straight into an explanation/description of what the session will look like, organize the players into teams, run a snappy warm-up to establish the right tone for what is to come, and start playing the game that has been described in the explanation of the session. This may change each week as the players improve, but the basic shape of this game can remain constant, whether it is a version of Tag Rugby, Rugby Netball, or a controlled and refereed game of touch.

The coach must not rush into the touch game until the players' skills are ready to cope. They must be capable of passing sideways while running forwards, so it may be best to keep to Tag or Rugby Netball until their passing skills are able to cope with touch. Once you do take the game on, ensure that numbers are kept to a minimum, and try to have fewer defenders than attackers so that scoring occurs frequently.

Starting the Session with Touch Rugby

Such a game of touch rugby is an ideal way to get a game going at the start of a session for players of all ages, and can help to establish a working tone. Avoid a game that is a players' recreational and social chat period: the worst preparation/introduction to any training session is to let the players 'run' their version of touch – a loose game such as this will almost certainly send out all the wrong messages, as it will not create a working atmosphere. The game suggested must be refereed, and the players will gain enormously from it once they start to appreciate that it is competitive, demanding, and likely to stretch their skills.

Touch rugby is played according to the following rules:

- Pitch size can be any dimensions to suit the number of players, but the coach should try to keep teams small in number. If there are too many players for something like six-a-side, have two games and all the coaches should be used to referee
- One of the defending team simply touches the opponent who has the ball with a sensible weighted touch with one hand
- The player who has been touched then faces the opponents' goal line and restarts play by rolling the ball back between his feet, which are astride but by no more than one metre
- The player who is rolling the ball may not pick the ball up at that stage; his side is allowed six touches before possession is handed over

- The player who picks up the ball from the roll is called the 'dummy half', but it can be a different player each time
- The defenders must be 5m back from the roll restart, and 10m back from a penalty restart

Possession is turned over with a roll ball when:

- the ball is dropped by the attacking team
- the dummy half is touched (by a player who came from an on-side position) in possession
- there have been six touches
- the roll ball has been incorrectly performed
- a tap penalty is performed incorrectly (see later)
- a player in possession steps on or over the touch line

The Tap Restart Penalty

This penalty is played as follows: one player places the ball on the ground, releases it with both hands, then taps it with either foot no further than one metre before picking it up to restart the game. Defenders must be 10m back from this restart.

A tap penalty restart is awarded for the following reasons:

- A forward pass
- A player in the attacking team rolling the ball before a touch has been made
- The roll ball was not made on the mark
- Any too robust a touch: there must be minimal force
- Claiming a touch that clearly had not been made
- Any number of defenders offside (not 5m) at the roll ball
- Any number of defenders offside at a tap restart (not 10m)
- Deliberately delaying play
- Obstruction

Once the players understand the game's requirements, the coach must referee the defence and insist that they retreat the correct distance after each restart. This makes the defending team work really hard as a unit, but they soon appreciate the importance of working hard together in a single line to get back to where the referee wants them; of not giving penalties away, and how that can be achieved through team discipline; and of listening to what the referee demands, and trying hard to deliver it. And when the defence is working legally and together, the attacking options will start to appear, and handling skills will flourish because there will be space that never existed in their own game of touch where the defenders are not working as a team.

Development in this game may be tried at a surprisingly early age, and one of these is the offload.

The Offload

The offload is regarded as an advanced skill, but it can easily be encouraged in this type of game of touch. One way this can be done is the coach calls 'touch' at any time before a legitimate touch is made: the ball carrier must slow down immediately, and on the call of a support runner coming from depth, plays the ball softly to the side for that support player to collect. This makes depth a pre-requisite, and the players might just absorb a valuable rugby lesson without feeling that it has been coached.

There can be further development on the call 'touch' again: the ball carrier slows, and the player touching him wraps his arms around his waist – but does not tackle him. The offload is again executed to a player who comes from depth and calls for the pass.

The next stage in the offload can be much later in players' progress and might be a live tackle in a small-sided game in a confined space where the pace is kept intentionally slow. The offload pass can be given at any time from the start of the tackle to the player in possession hitting the floor.

The pass should always be two-handed if possible, and the ball should not be hurled at the receiver: it needs to be a soft pass, a lifting action, that invites the receiver on to it.

Starting the Session with an Introductory Phase

Some coaches might be happier and more comfortable starting the session with an introductory phase, and there are many activities that will set a workmanlike tone before any small team games or coaching begin. Others may prefer to launch straight into a game – but spare the players the monotony of running endless circuits around the pitch: this is usually the sign of a coach desperately searching for time to plan the session in his mind, or one who is trying hard to use up as much time as possible – but if the players wanted coaching in middle-distance running technique they would have joined the athletics club. They want to play rugby.

The following handling exercises may help with an introductory phase if you feel you need one, but try to develop your own confidence so that you can get the game(s) going as early as possible in the session.

Whatever is used, plan to keep the players as close as possible, and keep it simple. The aim is to create a good working atmosphere while handling as much as possible.

Working in Pairs with One Ball per Pair

Mark the working area clearly and work in short bursts (30–60sec), with rest periods in between that can be used for coaching advice. The players move around the grid, and the exercise proceeds in the following way:

- The players pass to each other while moving, avoiding any collisions (by keeping their heads up)…
- …and increase the pace as competency improves
- The coach asks all players to move into the biggest space available (however far away it seems in the grid) when passing or receiving…
- …and keeps stressing the W shape of the receiver's hands, and the sympathetic pace on the pass
- Each player must let his partner know exactly where he is by effective communication
- On a call or signal from the coach, each player must find a different working artner and continue passing and/or receiving

The same activity can then be developed into one where scanning and 'heads up' become even more important. This exercise is the same as the one above, but with only two touch-lines, marked out with cones or poles to form a 90-degree angle. The other two lines are imaginary and are formed by the coach moving with his arms out. The players must be aware of where their support players are, and where the two constantly changing touch-lines are sited: this encourages them to be aware of the ball and the ever-changing space that is available.

Contact Work

This work can then be turned into a short, sharp period of contact work. Be aware that this is very tiring indeed, and the coach needs to work in very short bursts. There will be others working in the grid so the same message applies – move into a space when you get the ball.

- The ball carrier slows down when he takes the ball, crouches, and invites his partner to run in low to work the ball away
- The ball should be presented so as to invite the runner to come in low
- The low running must start a few paces from the ball carrier, and should not be a dropping action on to the ball in the final pace
- The new ball carrier moves a few paces away, and the process continues
- The coach must encourage shoulders and elbows to lead the movement for possession, and not the fingers

Coach – moving to change two touchlines.

Coach – moving to change two touch-lines.

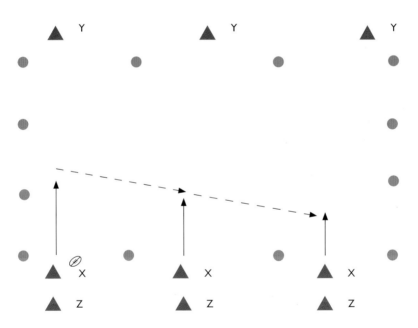

Continuous relays.

When the skill is improving, ask the ball carriers to add something more than token resistance so that the incoming player has to work a bit harder each time to secure possession.

Continuous Relays

These relays are fairly simple to set up, and all players can handle regularly and often. The basic set-up would be with three teams of three players, and the movement keeps going as long as the coach decides.

- Team X starts and passes the ball across the line
- The end player passes (softly) to the end player in front of him in team Y

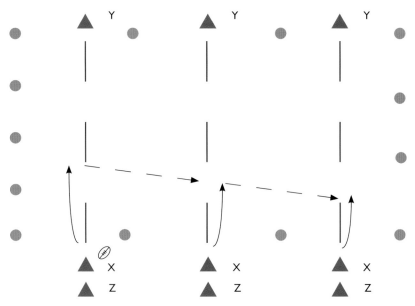

Poles added to continuous relays.

- Team Y passes and gives the ball to team Z

The purpose of the relay is to have a maximum period of intensive handling practice in the shortest time possible.

Do not make the playing area so wide that the players cannot pass comfortably, and keep changing the direction of the pass and the order of the players.

There are variations that can easily be added: instead of *passing* to the next team, roll the ball along the ground; or poles could be placed in the middle of the playing area so that players have to cope with passing and evasion.

The coach can replace the poles in the middle and so present a challenge to each group as they come across the playing area: this then involves decision-making for the ball carrier.

Once the players are doing well, have little

competitions and see who can do so many repetitions in a certain time. There are many variations on this theme and you will work out what is best for you.

When the players have improved, change their starting point: this obliges them to work hard to gain a support/handling role.

Mirroring

Though there is no ball work involved, mirroring can have a valuable role to play in the introduction to practice sessions, from absolute beginners to adult club players.

The coach faces the players, who have sideways and forward/backward space in case somebody gets it wrong. The coach simply moves and changes his sideways movements (left to right, right to left), and the players have to copy. They must concentrate, and when they master what is being asked of them, dummy changes of direction can be introduced and the pace can be increased. The

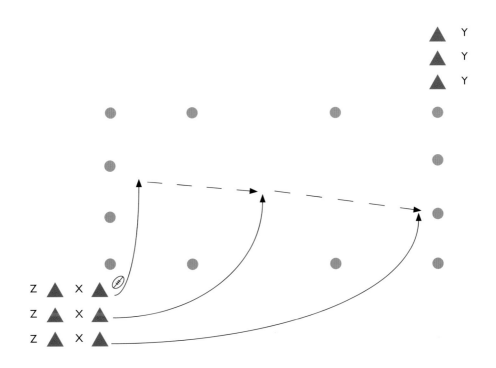

Changed starting positions for continuous relays.

players must be aware of what is in front of them (the coach is an opposing attacker!) and they have to concentrate on avoiding collisions.

Add forward/backward movements to the sideways ones. This will be more difficult to follow, so adjust the pace to suit the players' progress.

As a variation a player could take the coach's role, leaving the coach to help/comment on what the players are producing. Try to get them to watch the mover's hips and legs rather than his upper body: this is a valuable scanning skill that improves tackling.

Basic Technical Skills

Understanding the basic principles of the game

being played must never be forgotten, and the coach has a responsibility to understand the important concepts at the heart of rugby and how best to get them across through games *and* practices. All activity should have relevance to the game, and the work carried out in coaching should always impact on player improvement and the game itself.

Rugby is a complex game that must be simplified for the players being coached. The basic shape and techniques in the game are far removed from the relatively straightforward game of football. Many adults have probably had little formal coaching other than what they have picked up when playing the game, and younger players may never have seen a game.

Rugby coaches do need to work out the essentials of the game before they can get them across to their players, otherwise they

53

THE BASICS OF RUGBY

The game of rugby is played according to the following basic objectives and concepts:

- To win the ball and keep possession of it
- To keep the ball by supporting the ball carrier at all times
- Players are on their feet whenever possible
- The ball is off the ground and (as far as possible) is passed and received by hand
- Possession must take the team forwards (or there will never be a score). Players should have the mindset that they will always try to take the ball further forward than the point from which it was received – or a pass will be made to another player in a better position to allow that to happen
- Possession requires manipulation as there is not one single method of scoring, and spotting space(s) and getting a runner(s) into it is crucial
- Evasion is preferable to confrontation
- Whatever a player does has an effect on others in his team
- The talents of both individuals and team are required for success
- When defence is required, the same 'go forward' is an important part of it

will end up 'coaching' only through drills. The technical skills that drills can help with are enormously important, but they should not be an end in themselves: they are developed so they can have a part to play *in a game*.

Technical skills are very important and can be learned or improved in drills and practices if they do not emerge naturally in small team games. They eventually, however, have to be tested in a game (even if a conditioned game), and that leads into the requirement for players to understand *tactical* skills. *Tactical* skills are what you do with possession once you have it, and this is a far more complex area of the game.

Technical skills will be of great benefit in getting the ball and maintaining possession, but how best to use that possession takes the coach into how to develop players' awareness and intuition so that they sense what is a realistic/good option without having to think.

There are various practices in this section, but beware of using any of them before you have considered what you, as coach, want to achieve and what the players require. You

may end up aiming too high, and a useful bit of coaching advice is to remember the acronym KISS, which stands for 'Keep It Seriously Simple' or 'Keep It Simple, Stupid'.

There are thousands of drills and practices for rugby, but the effective coach will sift through them and select what is relevant for him and his squad at any given time. However, do try to avoid drills or practices just for the sake of doing them, and always ask yourself why you are doing something. Rugby is a game where practice sessions could consist solely of such drills without the players learning a single thing about the game itself. They might know how to give and take a pass after hours of practice, but there is little point in honing the skill if its relevance on the pitch is not understood. The effective coach will try to improve skills, and then bring them, at a pace that the players can cope with, into competition.

That competition does not, however, have to be a full game: it can be a small sided match, a conditioned game, or simply a practice against opponents and/or the stopwatch.

CHAPTER 5

HANDLING SKILLS

The most fundamental skill of all in the game of rugby is *handling* – giving and taking a pass. It sounds simple, but there will be a dramatically wide range of ability within any group, even in such a 'simple' skill. Many players will adopt the passing technique with little explanation, and they can be used to demonstrate this vital skill to others who are not so good at it.

There will come a point when passing skills will need attention; what players may well have absorbed and developed naturally in small-team games will require development and improvement. The practice work will cover many other skills that fall naturally into handling, because the skills in handling require so many other complementary skills at the same time. Players have to learn when and how to pass, and when and how not to pass; they must learn to scan for spaces, to identify what are the most productive lines of running, and how poor lines of running can destroy an attack.

Handling is basically one facet in passing and receiving; there are so many attendant considerations, so young and less able players, especially, need time to absorb the coaching lessons. The better players may pick it all up more quickly than the less able, but they will still need coaching attention and advice.

Giving a Pass

On receiving a pass, the ball is in the player's hands – with his fingers in the W position – his arms are coming from the side where the pass was received, with the elbows slightly bent, and his head is looking towards the player who is to receive the pass.

The player should use one sweeping movement across the body to transfer the ball to the next player's W-shaped hands. Squeeze the ball, especially with the thumbs, to maintain a secure grip on it until the pass has been given with a pushing motion.

A useful little practice for the coach is to have players moving around a coned area with half carrying a ball in front of them and away from the body. The other players try to knock the ball from any holder's grip. The player attempting to knock the ball out must use a flat palm, and must not make contact with anything other than the ball.

After the pass is given, the player should follow through with the hands and point them at the target. The ball should travel without any rotation in the air, in as close as possible to the vertical position. There should be no spin on the ball, though there will be a requirement later in the players' development for a spin pass over a longer distance *in the right circumstances.*

The player should concentrate on a sweeping/pushing motion of the arms, and not think of the leg strides. The usual pattern is for the left leg to be forward when taking a pass from the right, then the right leg goes forward with one stride when passing to the left. If this happens naturally, all is well.

Bent leg to gain distance in the pass.

There may be a player(s) who simply cannot co-ordinate this movement, and who may need individual or small-group attention. However, the majority will get it right from the outset and they should not be asked to think about a skill that has happened without thought. The coach should deal with the problem(s) separately.

Ideally, giving a pass is achieved in one movement. A good coaching point for young players is to imagine that there is a wall immediately in front of them and the ball must not move forwards into that wall; this keeps the hands close to the body.

The player should practise to execute the passing movement within a single stride.

One bad habit that young players may adopt in the early stages is to bend a knee and drop that hip to offer more leg power into the pass. The coach must look out for this, as the arm swing and wrist action must be encouraged. Dropping the left side of the body to pass to the right (and vice versa) will be detrimental to future progress in the player's passing skills.

It is important to emphasize 'soft hands' (as above).

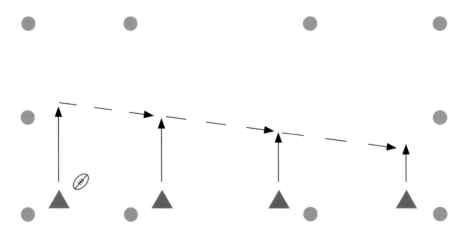

Holding the run to produce depth.

Receiving a Pass

Any player who is likely to receive a pass, or is in the near vicinity of the player in possession, should run with their hands held towards the ball with the fingers in the W position (thumbs just touching) and the arms slightly bent so that they allow a bit of 'give' when taking the ball. The W shape presents a target for the passer and helps him to spot exactly where the pass should go.

Once the receiver gets the ball he should accelerate as quickly as possible in as straight a line as possible and threaten the defensive line. Good coaching will suggest that the run ought to be timed *not* from when the ball starts a passing sequence, but from the actions and run of the player immediately inside. This is a difficult concept for many players, and their instinct will be to start running when the line starts.

However, the coach needs to give the players confidence in holding their sprint and taking a cue from the immediate inside player. If all the players in a line start to run

forwards at the first movement/pass, many of them will overrun the ball well before it gets to them, and they will either be in front of the ball and out of the game, or they will receive the ball without any space to give a pass. A useful practice is to follow this sequence:

- All four players start in a flat line
- The ball carrier (No. 1 in the diagram) moves forwards
- Only when No. 1 takes a step can No. 2 move and take a pass
- No. 3 must wait until No. 2 moves before he may go forwards
- No. 4 does the same

This can highlight the fact that players do not have to stand very deep to create depth, and depth can be created by the support players holding their run until the man inside moves.

Players should always catch the ball in front of the body, and not bring it back into the body – unless circumstances such as a tackle dictate otherwise.

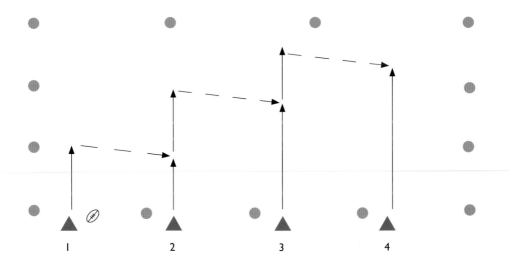

Running beyond where a player gets the ball.

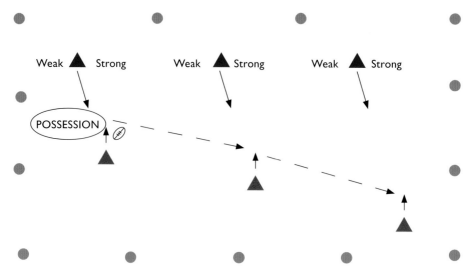

Weak and strong sides in defenders.

They should try to accelerate into and through the ball, though this is only possible when some depth has been maintained.

They should also try to run beyond the point from where the pass started. If the passes take each player further backwards, there will never be any forward progression and a try will never be scored.

Take a line of run slightly back into the ball. This is called 'cutting the pass', and is a valuable skill that allows a team/player to maintain the outside space whilst presenting the defender(s) with a tackle on their weak side.

The player should not fall away from the pass as it is taken, but should maintain the running line, which should be slightly back towards the ball.

He should try to watch the ball and any players/obstacles in front. Some players may put all their visual attention on the ball to better their chances of catching it, but later there will be defenders, and they need to practise so they see them as well as the pass.

The coach should encourage the awareness of 'soft hands' and keep emphasizing it. Many players grab for the ball, and this action can spill possession. Ask them to pass and take a pass with a degree of sympathy for the immediate player, and stress this in all practices and match situations.

Coaching Technical Skills

You, the coach, and the players have to appreciate that giving and taking a pass is not a skill in isolation, it is a building block towards playing the game with other players. Part of your coaching must be aimed at getting each skill as proficient as possible and using it to form part of a game. Skills are rarely closed, and do not exist in isolation from other team components; decision making and learning to adapt to what is around must be part of handling skill work.

OPEN AND CLOSED SKILLS

Open skills are skills that may have to be adapted in a changing environment – for example, passing to beat an opponent. Closed skills take place in a stable, predictable environment (such as snooker, or a free shot at basketball) and the skill is not affected by that environment – for example, place kicking. However, most rugby skills are open, because even the place kick will be affected by ground, weather and ball conditions.

The coach has to assist players in improving their technical skills while offering them practice opportunities and challenges so that they learn to make game decisions and adapt to what is required 'on the hoof'. There is little point in any player learning and developing a certain skill or competency for that skill's sake: there has to be an accompanying game-playing competence, which can be encouraged and improved alongside skill practice.

The coach must become aware that different players learn differently, and this may be at the root of some young players' problems with certain skills. Coaching rugby is no different from teaching in the classroom, and you soon learn that they, the players, are all different. There will be those who just need to be told what the skill is, and they will pick it up from your description. Some will need to see the skill being performed by other, more competent players. A video of the skill may be absorbed best. There are those who will need the pattern of the play/skill to be drawn on a board with arrows showing the line of run. And some will need a mixture of every visual and audio aid available.

That is the reality of coaching any players, but the coach must not assume that a certain player cannot pick up a certain skill – the truth may be that he cannot pick up that skill from the way it has been presented.

Once a skill practice or game has started, do not be afraid to stop it when a fault screams out for attention. There is little point in practising failure, but your intervention has to make sense to the players. If the majority are coping, let them play and deal separately with the few who are struggling. If you have to do this, keep a smile on your own face and do not let the majority think that the intervention is serious; you are simply trying to help players improve.

When it is appropriate, ask the players questions. Do not be afraid of letting them 'in' on the coaching: they are not a threat, and they are not taking your authority away. The effective coach will involve players' opinions in the coaching and development process as long as their input is constructive and at the right time when the activity stops for such discussion.

If you have an injured player, use him. He might be given a certain task to report back to you and the players on how they coped with a certain situation. He may not be very confident or very good at it, but players will improve with a bit of help from the coach. Encourage them to comment without that being a threat to their peers.

Try to make up your own games and skill practices. There is no right or wrong way to practise; there are blueprints of drills that can be adapted by the resourceful coach, and most players will enjoy variety on a single theme instead of doing the same thing time after time.

Activities to Practise and Improve Handling Skills

The elements of giving and taking a pass are central to achieving more than a game that consists mainly of stoppages through poor handling. The basic good habits apply to introductory 'fun' games just as much as when the players develop into requiring them in a proper game.

The Passing Procedure

The passing procedure is easily practised in continuous lines of runners. You can arrange the numbers to suit your requirements, but three or four a side is ample. Do stress what

you are looking for, and always maintain the coaching of hand positions in passing and receiving.

- Start slowly – half pace is fast enough to begin with, so that the skill is produced and the players get a feel for what is best practice
- Build up the pace while maintaining competence
- Ensure that the middle players switch position so that no one player is always first or last in the line
- Insist on retrieving the ball if it is dropped. Spilling possession does not mean that the game is over, and players should be aware that the ball on the floor must be

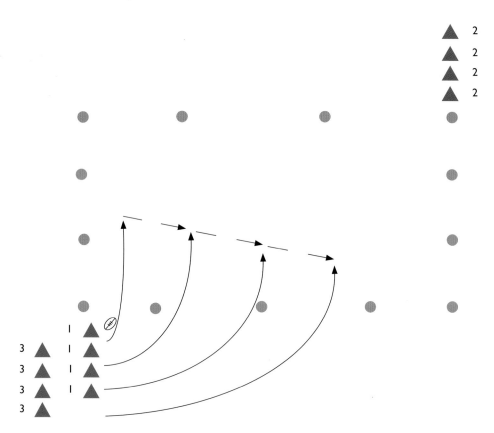

Continuous handling.

picked up and, if possible, at least another pass given. This is a very important mental discipline and should be a regular component in all skill work

- Get the end man to touch down to score each time. This is more game-related than popping up to the waiting group
- When the group is competent, add the stopwatch to see which group can carry out so many in a certain time; or get different groups to see which one can score so many tries first. Be aware that this is when the skills might disintegrate, so watch carefully for anything going wrong and keep reminding the players what the correct skill is.
- Always try to get the skill back into a conditioned game as soon as possible, so run a conditioned game or conditioned game of touch where players just concentrate on the passing and receiving elements.

Acting as a Support Runner

An important handling skill is to be willing to act as a support runner once the ball carrier has passed. As the groups handle and run towards the next group, get the first passer to run to the outside and act as the new last player in the line.

This may start as a difficult skill as that first man must not drift across (towards the direction in which he will run after the pass) before his pass. His natural instinct will be to move towards the end of the passing movement before and during his pass, but this will automatically take the outside space that good handling techniques are trying to maintain. He must initiate forward momentum by starting his run straight at where the defence would be.

This addition to the skill will emphasize the need to see the game as more than a

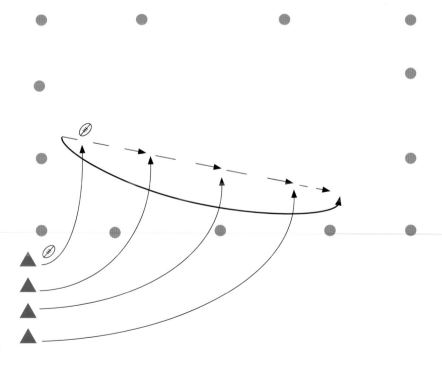

Adding an 'extra' player.

single action, and it will test the players in their efforts to get to the end and 'cut' the ball when they get there.

If you are running groups of four or more and the players understand the concept and are producing the skill correctly and regularly, test them further by getting the first two in the line to support on the outside.

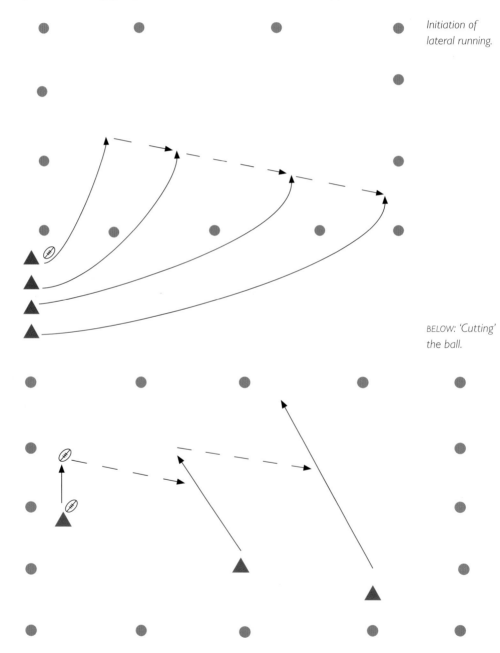

Initiation of lateral running.

BELOW: 'Cutting' the ball.

First two runners supporting outside.

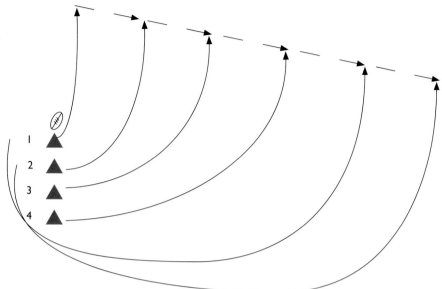

Do make sure that you arrange the practices so that you give equal time to left- and right-handed passing. It is very easy to restrict the practice to left-to-right sequences.

Developing the Scrum-half Pass

Any of the practices can be useful to develop the scrum-half pass. The players at scrum-half can start off each passing sequence, and the coach will be learning about which players can pass off either hand in the scrum-half role.

Do not let your recognized scrum-half make all these passes. Other players might be required to act in that position during a match, and they all need the confidence from practice sessions to know that they can cope if the scrum-half is out of the game.

Coping with Lateral Movement

The players will never get the perfect running lines at all times, so it is worthwhile getting them to have strategies to cope with lateral movement when it occurs. These can be built into your handling practices by asking a player

to drift across intentionally during the practice to see who can react and straighten the line.

Strategies to straighten up the line when it moves laterally include the scissors pass and the dummy scissors.

Scissors Pass

Once the ball carrier starts to drift across, the nearest player outside him should recognize this and take a scissors ball to straighten the line. The passer must face the taker all through the motion of passing so that he can see the receiver at all times, and he will not present a painful area to the defenders when a tackle arrives.

The decision to call for a scissors pass may best be made by the widest player (wing) or the deepest (full back). Once either has recognized the lateral attacking line, an authoritative call has to be made for a strategy to put the fault right.

The Dummy Scissors

That call itself may disorganize the defence,

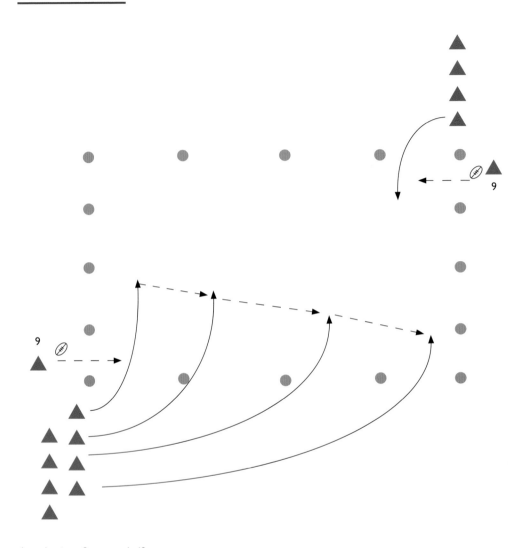

Introduction of a scrum-half.

and a dummy scissors could then be the best option. The pass is not given, though the second player in the scissors must run a line that suggests that he will be taking the scissors pass.

The ball carrier shows the ball to suggest that the scissors will be executed, then keeps running without giving that pass.

Whoever ends up with the ball from the scissors or the dummy scissors must accept responsibility for going straight and towards the try line at pace.

Practising the Scissors (or Switch)

There are four main exercises of increasing complexity that will practise the scissors pass, as described below.

Exercise 1: Work in a channel (5m width is ample, between touch and 5m line) so that

The scissors.

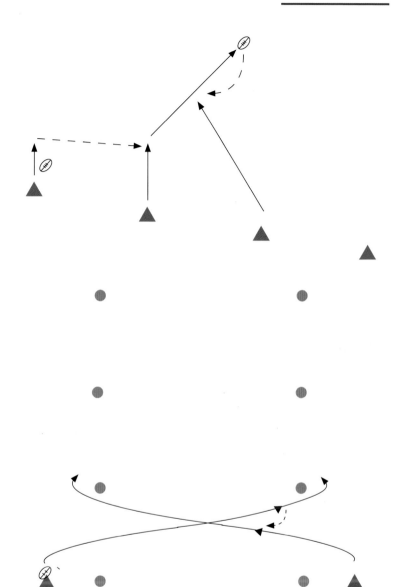

Practising the scissors (pairs).

the players do not have to run too far each time. Work in pairs, and aim to give/take the scissors in the middle of the grid. Make sure the ball is being gripped, and look for the partner's hands (W shape and held up), which are the target. Pivot at the hips, gradually turning the back to where a defender would be, and give a soft pass slightly ahead of the receiver

so that he does not have to slow up to collect it.

Exercise 2: This can then develop into the same two-player switch, but each player keeps running out to the side line (touch and the 5m line) before starting the movement again, thus keeping the switching movement going.

65

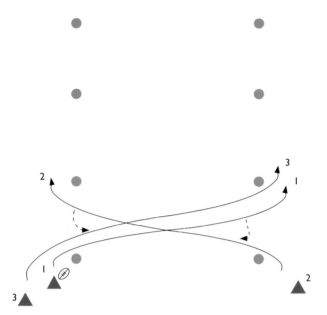

Practising the scissors (threes).

persevere with something that is baffling to the majority.

Exercise 3: Next you can play a three-player switch in a 10m channel (between the 5m and 15m lines). The middle player starts and switches with an outside player. All players run to an outside line before turning in for the next switch.

Exercise 4: Four-player switch (between touch and the 15m line). Marker cones or poles must be used so that players can see where they are going, and you must walk through this before building up speed. The sequence is 1 2, 2 3, 3 4. Players 1 and 2 must run wide of their cone to allow the immediate runners in near the cone.

Practices 3 and 4 may be baffling for the less able players, so do not introduce them without thought and considerable build-up practice. If the players don't understand it, don't be afraid to go back a stage(s), or just leave it and use it at a later date. You want your players to be successful, so do not

Progression: the Flat Pass

In this pass both players run forwards before the ball carrier cuts across. The receiver reacts to his line of run only when he has started to move sideways and forwards, then goes as before.

Much more difficult is the flat pass with the next runner cutting the pass to straighten the line of running. Again, this requires an outside player to recognize that the possession is going sideways: he has to call for the flat pass as he cuts back slightly and takes that pass.

In a further progression the *full back enters the line* and straightens the line of run.

Or the *dummy scissors* could be used, and the full back enters the line from depth.

It is relatively straightforward to play a conditioned game where the coach nominates a player to run laterally so that the others can learn to recognize the fault and implement a remedy. However, there is a danger that the players will then try scissors and flat pass moves at all times instead of simply concentrating on the basic skill of straight running lines that hold the defence. The coach must make it clear to the players that these strate-

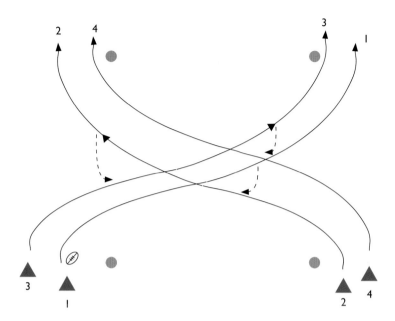

Practising the scissors (fours).

gies are to rectify previous errors, and are not to be used just to show that the players can produce them.

If, in this process, the coach finds a person who can naturally and simultaneously cut a pass *and* hit a space, you have found a most valuable player. Taking a pass while hitting a space is one of the game's real line-breakers, and it should be encouraged in all practice sessions and/or games of touch.

Playing from any Situation

Once the players show a fair degree of competence, make the skill even more game-related by having them start from anything but straight lines, both in practices and in conditioned games. In a live match, players rarely pass or receive the ball in a controlled environment, so an early lesson is to play from any situation.

Players need to learn to adapt to what is happening, and to accept that what is planned does not always occur in a game. They also need to run in support, and the following little practices can add some support work.

In the first practice, the first player passes,

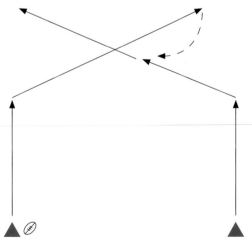

Scissors – progression to the flat pass.

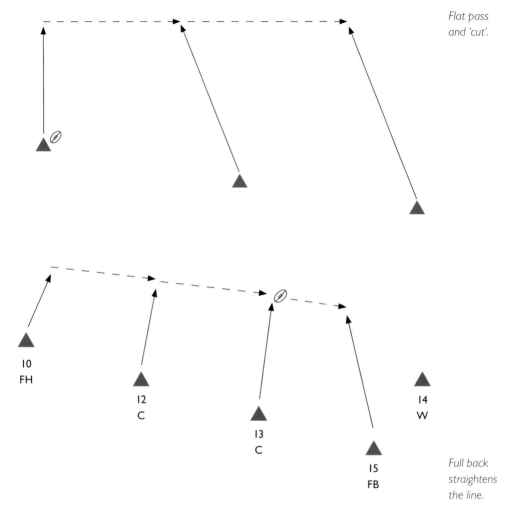

Flat pass and 'cut'.

10
FH

12
C

13
C

14
W

15
FB

Full back straightens the line.

then covers across to support and score on the outside. The tendency for this player is to start the support run (sideways) before or during the pass. However, the coach must direct the players to run forwards and pass before the change of direction to support on the outside, otherwise the sideways early movement will nullify what the players are trying to achieve, and the outside space will be eroded as the whole line slides across; in a match situation this will make the defenders' job easier.

This is very much a confidence skill – being aware that the first line of run will nearly always condition and affect what happens next. Players tend to think of the game within their own area of participation, so the effective coach will always try to get across how important it is to hit the correct line to get a positive result later in the sequence of play.

Once the players have accepted the coaching points and are regularly producing the skills with a fair degree of competence on a regular basis, a second exercise could be

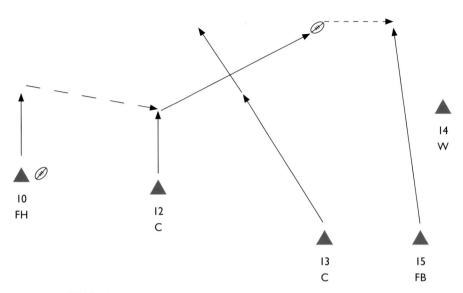

Dummy scissors and full back in.

First passer covers across to score.

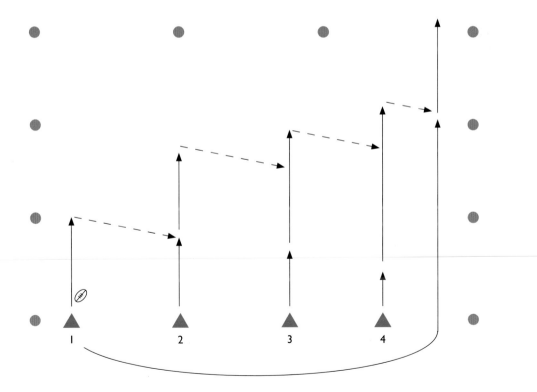

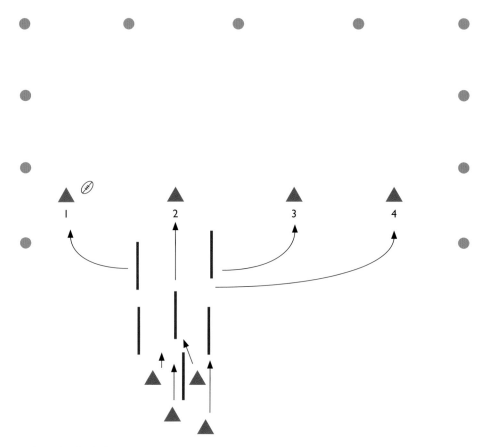

Running through poles before passing.

to change the starting point and who goes where by running each group through a set of poles before the handling starts. The set-up is the same as above, but the teams get through the poles before the handling begins. The fastest runner may automatically become the first passer at all times, so ask him to hold back or go around an extra pole if this is happening.

To avoid this, you can have the coach toss the ball to one player when they are in the middle of the poles, and he has to start the practice off at a given mark as before. If you do not have enough poles, use tackle shields on the ground, but watch the players carefully

because they will quickly learn that it is very easy to run straight over the obstacles.

Once the players have gained competency at the skills and obstacles, add another dimension to the skill by starting the groups from standing behind each other, rather than at the side.

The same 'extras' can be added with poles, and this starts players thinking about the following:

- Depth of support
- Slowing slightly when giving the pass
- Running 'through' the ball

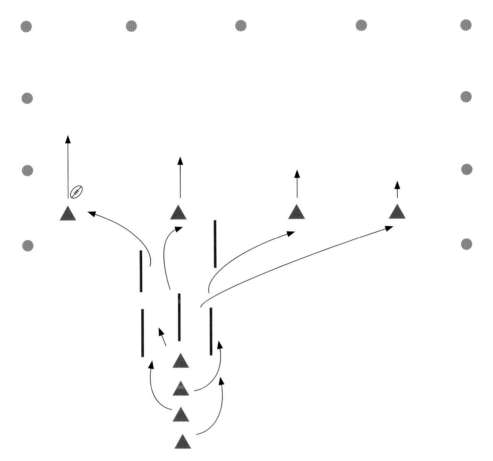

Indian file before running through poles.

- Taking possession further forward than from where it was received
- Telling the ball carrier where you are with a clear signal of when and how you want the pass

Some players may need to go back a stage, and this can be done easily in a practice to make them aware of what needs to be done to get to the ball when they have not started from where they hope to be. This practice proceeds as follows:

- Four (or five) players line up as in the diagram
- On the coach's call the ball is passed along the line after a pass from 9, who runs behind the attackers to get to the next ball
- The players must complete the passing before they reach the outer line of the grid, and the final player must receive the ball inside cone 2
- The final player scores at (or just inside) cone 2

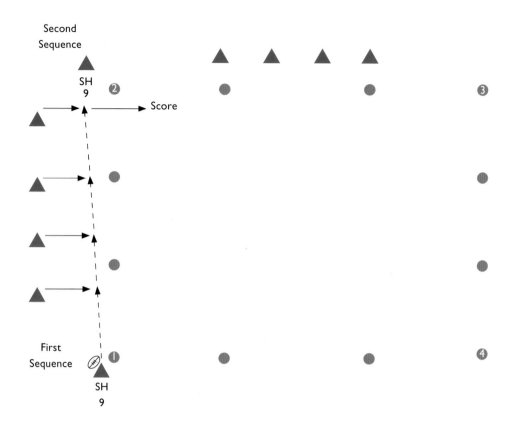

Working hard to find a running line.

- The players realign on cone 2, and the passing practice is repeated until a score is made back at cone 3

Progression: The same practice is carried out from a far more difficult starting point. The players stand in Indian file and have to work very hard to get to where the pass will be. The sequence is the same as before, but the players are now asked to produce effective running lines and handling skills when they have come from very deep to begin the process.

Depth in Attack

Depth in attack is a complex subject. It is simple to talk about, but once players get into the heat of a game it is one of the first things to disappear. A common question will be: how deep is deep? Probably the best answer is to suggest that support players should be able to see the number on the ball carrier's back (or where the number would be if he had one).

There is practice work that can be done, and players must be coached to appreciate the value of a player(s) coming on to a flat line

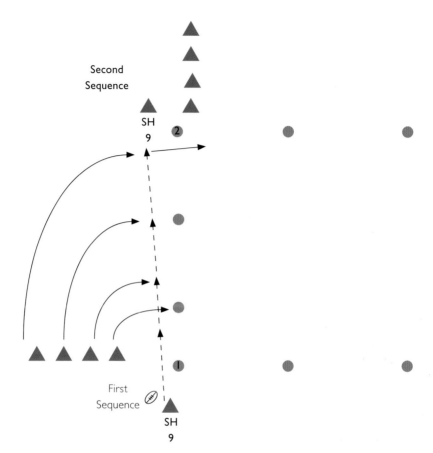

Starting in Indian file before finding a running line.

of attack. It is a concept that is well worth the coaching time spent, and players will see the benefits when they realize that a player from depth can add real go-forward to the game – and there is the bonus that defenders will find it difficult to spot a runner coming into the game from depth.

The practice proceeds as follows:

- The players are in groups of three, and start on both sides of the channel (15m wide)
- On a signal, group 1 runs back, receives the ball from the feeder, then turns and attacks down the 15m channel, where all three handle

- At the same time, group 2 runs around their cone and trails group 1. As the third man in group 1 takes the pass, the second group calls for a pass, then runs through from depth. All three players in group 2 handle

Developments:

- Group 1 holds depth after they pass to group 2, then runs through group 2 and handles again
- Defenders can be introduced from the side of the channel so the attackers must look up at all times as well as passing

All the basic elements that have been coached

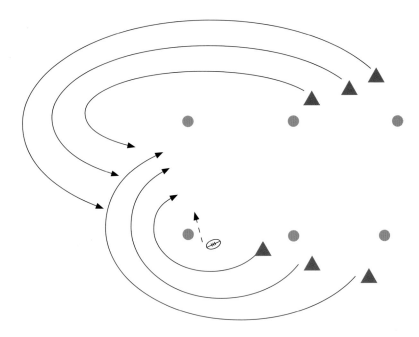

Depth practice.

Depth practice with defenders.

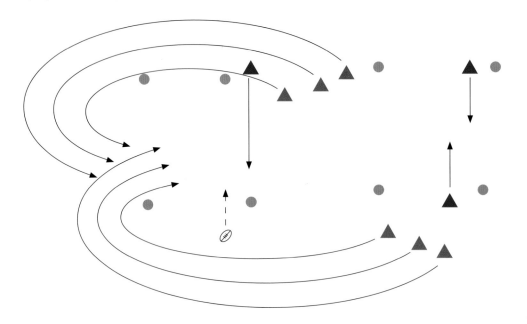

previously must be watched so that players do not regress in their skills. Do not practise incompetency and lazy habits; your attention to detail will help the players later.

COACHING STYLE

The coach must adopt a coaching style that is helpful and moderate. The last thing any player wants is to have his weakness bawled out in front of the rest, so work on this as hard as your players work on their playing skills.

Questioning is an important element for the coach in all skill work, but try to develop a non-threatening method of getting feedback. Players, whatever their age or experience, will not respond to the 'Why did you do that, you idiot?' tone of interrogation. They may respond better to a 'Could you think of what went wrong and how might it be improved?' tone, and this is an important area of coaching. You want to develop your players to think and have an opinion; your style of questioning is a skill and must be regarded as a tool that you must work on every bit as hard as the players practise.

During any of this skill work, the coach can stand in the middle of the relays and generally get in the way so that players develop the skill of when **not** to pass. However, you are not there to deliberately stop the practice; you are just adding a defender's body so that the players have to think about that while performing the skill. When done properly and sympathetically, this can add to the fun element – though beware of becoming the main part of the activity. Do not get carried away with your own tally of interceptions!

These passing skills have to stand the test of opposition, and a vital component of the pass is how to use it to beat another player. However, you do not have to keep rigidly to passing practices, and then into beating an opponent – there will inevitably be an element of mix and match, and you may decide that it is right for players to learn about how to pass to beat an opponent before, during or after the handling work. You have to decide what will suit your players best at a given time.

The Test of Opposition

Too often in rugby the sight of a line of opponents in a defensive wall results in the attack driving straight into the nearest defender. But there are ways to move and manipulate such a defence. This often happens close to a breakdown when one side has managed to recycle the ball – only to be confronted by a solid wall of defenders.

Too often the attackers take the ball straight into the nearest defender, thus handing the initiative to that defence. But it does not have to be like that, and a coaching aim might be to get players to manipulate the space, however small, in front of them. This practice needs to be carried out regularly so that it becomes second nature to all players in the squad, especially the forwards who will probably be faced with this scenario most often on the edges of a breakdown.

Walk through the process so that distinct patterns start to emerge, and encourage your players to think 'evasion' rather than 'confrontation'. The solid wall in front of them will have weaknesses, which must be exploited.

Stage 1
- Attacker 1 (A1) attacks the space between the two red cones
- Just before he reaches the cones, he steps into the space between cones to his left or right

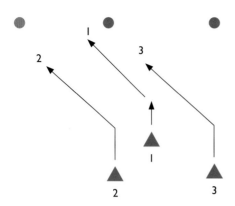

Manipulate the space – stage 1.

- The two support runners mirror this movement
- This encourages the support players to hold depth, as they do not know which side A1 will go
- It also improves silent communication, as support players must scan for signs rather than verbal communication on the direction of play

Stage 2

- The blue cones are scrum-half players, and a shield has been introduced to show the position of a likely defender

- A1 receives a pass from a nominated scrum-half, and aims for the shield (a defender)
- He steps away and goes with the direction of the pass to attack the outside defender; A2 and A3 mirror his movement
- A1 then has the option of passing to the outside support player, or popping the ball back to the inside support runner

Stage 3

- There are now four shields: three form a flat first-up defence, and the fourth

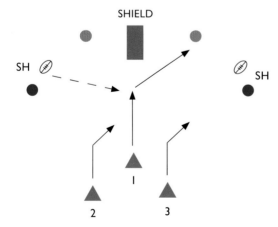

Manipulate the space – stage 2.

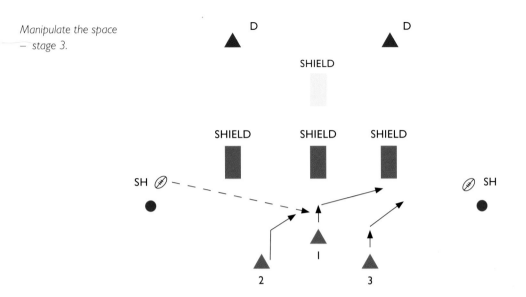

Manipulate the space — stage 3.

(yellow) is held by the coach. Two defenders are added deeper than the shield held by the coach

- A1 receives a scrum-half pass and attacks the middle shield
- A1 then steps sideways (in the direction of the pass) to meet that outside defender; A2 and A3 mirror the movement
- The shield that is being confronted comes to meet A1, and he passes to the attacker on his outside, alternatively the shield tries to cover the support attacker and A1 goes through
- Then the yellow shield comes in to pressurize the ball carrier, and a pass is made to beat that shield
- The ball carrier takes on the two deeper defenders and runs straight at the space between them

- Support players hold depth and react to the ball carrier's line of run while giving him support on both sides

When the ball is taken to the space between these defenders, the three attackers have the advantage.

- If the defenders do not come in to meet the ball carrier and they guard the support runners, there is a space between them to run at
- If one or both move to meet the ball carrier, there has to be one side where a pass will be to a support runner in space

CHAPTER 6

DEVELOPING AND IMPROVING HANDLING SKILLS

Even if the coach adopts a game-centred approach to coaching, there will be a need at some time to isolate a certain skill and work on it. However, rugby is a complex game and there are few 'closed' skills that can be isolated; place kicking, restarts and the throwing-in technique at the line-out can be practised as 'closed' skills, but once running, handling and opposition tackles come into the equation there is little hope of identifying 'closed' skills.

If a weakness (whether group or individual) is identified, the practice to improve it will require players who are already competent (and who may become bored quickly) and a range of practices that require other competencies so that the 'weakness' can be worked on.

There will always be a wide range of ability in your groups, so the way you develop practices is vitally important so that the weaker player(s) can improve while the better players feel that they are being challenged and are still developing their own skills.

Some of your players may already find the game complex, so be very careful not to become too fussy on breaking it down into very minute segments. If this occurs you will forever be running sessions of drills: better to try to involve the players in conditioned games to get your coaching across.

However, there will be a need to coach skills in practices away from the game. Once you start a period of such work, ensure that the content is relevant to the players' needs; avoid working them on a 'good' drill that you have just picked up because they will soon work out what you are doing.

Then ensure that player boredom does not creep in: in your planning, make the practice short and sharp with small numbers working to get maximum activity. If players have to wait too long to get into the practice, their minds may wander because they soon learn to guesstimate how long it might be before they will be active. Keep them all active, interested, alert, and aware of the need to concentrate.

Passing to Beat an Opponent

The key elements of passing and catching are still vitally important, yet some players will quite naturally (and without any coaching) beat an opponent. Value these skills if you are lucky enough to have such a player, but accept that there are other times in a game when a formal structure and system is required to break down a defence. The solo run to score is laudable, but often the team requires a passing movement between a number of players to achieve success.

Two versus One (2 v 1)
Start with an activity like this and you will quickly find out who understands the first concept of attacking a defence.

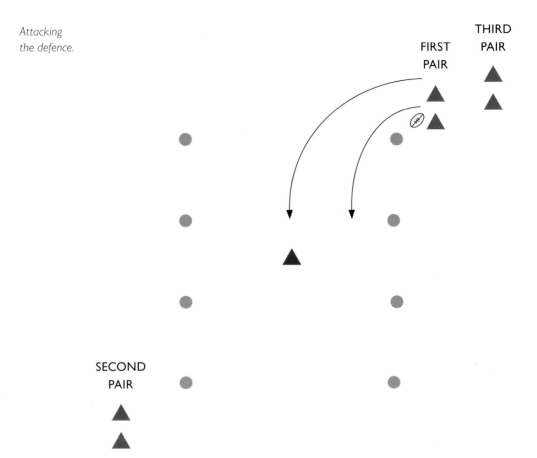

*Attacking
the defence.*

- Work in a channel no wider than 10m
- Arrange players in pairs and build up a continuous relay, but remember to change teams and the defender around
- Keep altering the direction of pass so that players are not always practising one way

The players enter the field of play and the ball carrier immediately runs quickly on a line between the two poles. Even if the defender is not on that line, he keeps to it and scores if the defender stays outside him.

If, however, the defender does stay on the attacker's line of run, he takes a line on the defender's inside shoulder to 'fix' him. You can become very theoretical about this, but the purpose of the run towards the defender's inside shoulder is to hold him from a covering defensive run after the pass.

The first attacker must develop an awareness of when the defender is 'fixed', and this will be best achieved by practising the skill many times. Some will grasp the concept immediately, while others will need coaching to help them to achieve awareness and competence.

The inside and outside shoulders are named depending on where the ball came from, and there is a critical point in the defender's stance that requires explanation to many players.

If the defender is 'fixed' his weight will be on his inside leg and an accurate and well

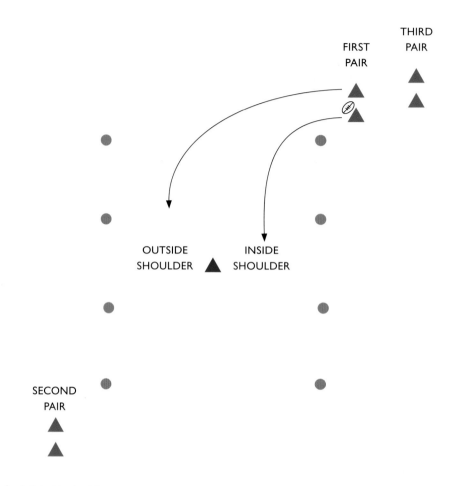

THIRD PAIR

FIRST PAIR

OUTSIDE SHOULDER   INSIDE SHOULDER

SECOND PAIR

ABOVE: Defender's inside shoulder.

BELOW: Inside and outside shoulder.

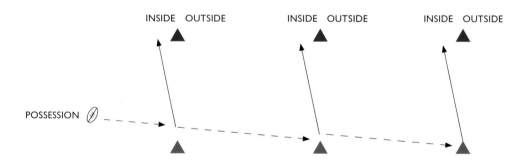

INSIDE   OUTSIDE   INSIDE   OUTSIDE   INSIDE   OUTSIDE

POSSESSION

timed pass will take him completely out of the game.

However, if that defender is not 'fixed' and is hedging his bets on whether to defend or hold off, the ball-carrier should keep running quickly at the inside shoulder line. A pass to a support runner will probably be tackled by the defender who is not 'fixed'. The ball-carrier should simply keep running if that defender does not come in, because any tackle that is made will be on the defender's weaker side and the runner will probably break that attempted tackle.

The coach may need diagrams to explain the concept to those who do not pick this up naturally. Many players feel that there is something inherently wrong with running at a space on the inside shoulder of the immediate defender, and they are often attracted to the best defended areas after a sideways run

with the ball. Coach competence in this area and you will have mastered one of the game's most baffling concepts for many players of all ages.

There can be a fun element to this coaching, and the nominated defender can add to it by trying to baffle the attackers with his own changing lines of defence for each set of attackers. At this stage it is probably best to defend with a two-handed touch tackle, but the coach may add a live tackle with the

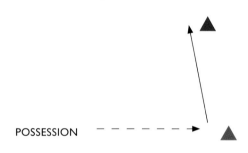

POSSESSION

TOP: 'Fixing' a defender.

MIDDLE: 'Fixing' a defender then passing.

BOTTOM: Weak and strong sides at tackle.

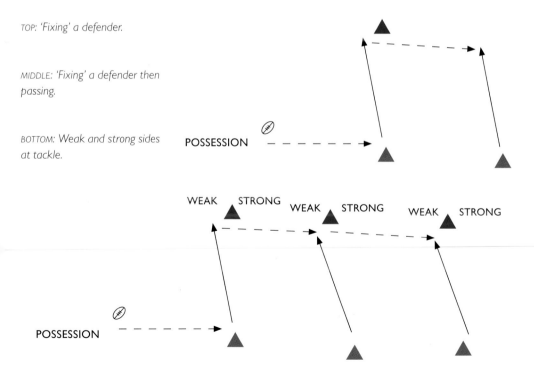

protection of a tackle suit. If this happens, do make sure that the defender changes regularly, as you do not want one player to tackle over and over again because you have lost track of how long he has been there. Limit this role by time or by a set number of sequences from the attack.

Three versus Two (3 v 2)

The progression from 2 v 1 takes players into a very difficult part of the game. Once you venture into 3 v 2, your main coaching job is to convince the players that the same principles apply, and they have to be convinced that this is 2 v 1 twice over. Once the first runner starts things on the correct line of run, the skills become easier; if he starts laterally, there is little chance of success.

One major coaching point is to get players to run straight ahead if there is a space – even though the player may have seen spaces on the outside. This means that the outside runners have to work back to the ball carrier's line of run to offer close support, but

that generally becomes more effective than the ball carrier looking for other players' spaces.

There is a practice that can be tried when the players' competencies are up to it. (The coach is at the heart of all the work and he decides on the pace of things.) It is organized as follows:

- There are three attackers each time, and they run backwards around a cone before the first runner takes the coach's pass to attack
- As the attackers start, two defenders run backwards around their entry cone before they come in to defend
- You can have one single line of players and they take turns to go off as three attackers versus two defenders. Or you can nominate two sets of two defenders and they alternate for so many times each
- The attackers may not pass back or introduce a scissors move. All passes must be towards the open side of each play

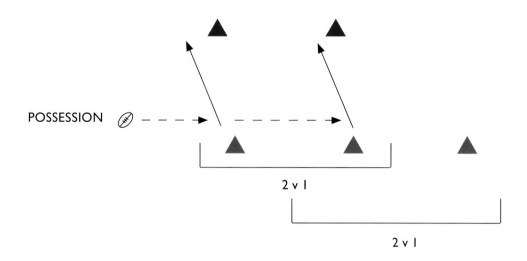

3 v 2.

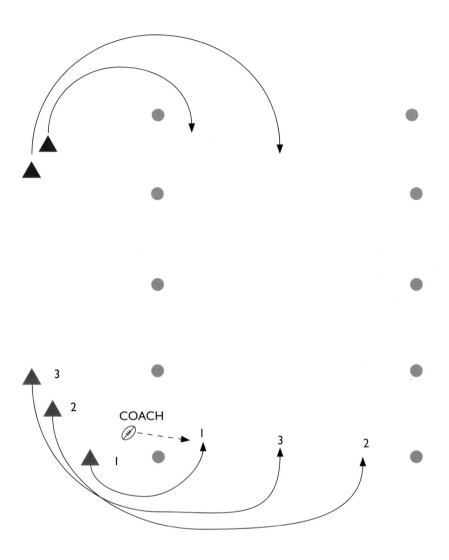

3 v 2.

- The first attacker is the ball carrier and he *must* hold his line close to the two cones (the touchline) to hold the defence in. If he drifts across, the defence will win
- The second attacker runs as wide as he can to draw the second defender

- The third attacker comes between one and two

There are various potential scenarios, and the players have to look up and watch the shape of the defence:

- If the first defender does not stay on the first attacker, the latter just runs through to score
- If the second defender goes wide to the third attacker, the second attacker shoots into the space and calls for the pass
- If the second defender stays on the second attacker, the outside third attacker calls for the ball

This practice contains many elements that all players need. The first attacker's role becomes the hardest for many players, but it is worth persevering with it because it affects backs in full flight and forwards in handling in cramped conditions.

The defenders can play two-hand touch rules, but you can eventually make it live tackling in tackle suits when that becomes appropriate. Don't be afraid to place a couple of players at the end of the practice (facing the attackers) and ask them to report on why an attempt succeeded or failed; this reinforces the coaching message very quickly and avoids the whinge that 'the coach is always getting at me'. There is nothing like a little peer appraisal to show that you might just be right!

Once the players appreciate the skills, you can get the defenders to defend in different ways. They could defend with the outside player up first, they could scissors then defend, or they could both target one player. One thing you, as coach, should ask them to do occasionally is *not* to defend. They could aim at space or simply both run to the outside attacker at the same time. You will be surprised how many attacking players will not see this, even though it is happening before their very eyes – and this trans-

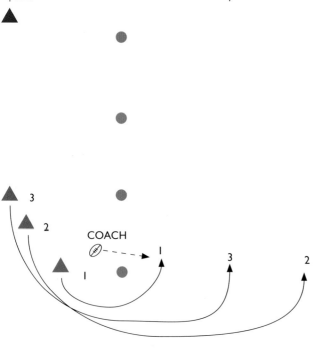

First defender goes wide.

Second defender wide.

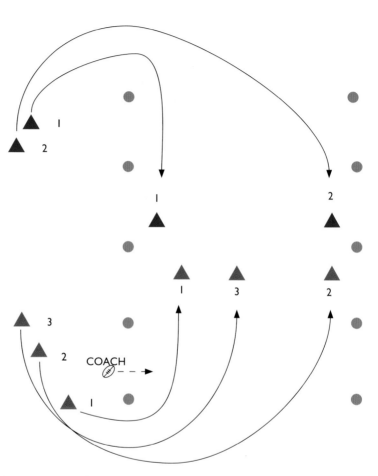

lates into poor decision making in matches because the ball carrier has not appreciated what the defence is up to.

So condition your players to play what they see in front of them: if there is no defender, run straight and score; if there is a defender, hold him in and pass to a support player. It sounds too simple to be true, but it is a core part of the game that so many players simply cannot cope with, yet we churn out moves, ploys and complicated strategies when they haven't yet learned the ABC. Do not become tempted to paste over the cracks of skill deficiency with over-elaboration and moves. And if you have to have strike/set moves, practise aborting in the middle if it is not going to plan or a better option presents itself. A called move does not mean that it has to be followed through to the end – it is merely an indication of where you want to go if the opposition agree to the script.

This practice allows all the basic skills of handling, giving and taking a pass, lines of running, depth of the attack, decision making, spotting space and calling instructions to be practised in a relatively small area. The coach is at the centre of all the activity and he can stop it at any time to discuss what has happened and what needs to happen with the players involved.

There is often a good case for using an existing line on the pitch to show the first player's most effective line of run; if there is no whitewashed line, place a line of cones so that the players are given a physical target on the ground as well as the inside shoulder of the first defender to aim for.

The handling skills of the players can be put to the test with some fitness-related practice, but the coach must intervene if the skill element is being eroded with slack passing. The players must concentrate through all of the time allotted.

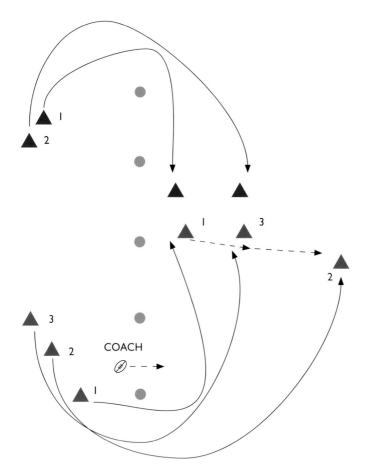

Both defenders mark first two attackers.

Time the activity and see which group can score most tries in the time allowed.

This activity gives an opportunity for handling, spotting spaces, drawing defenders, support and scoring. It can become very tiring and can quickly have an aerobic element, so do allow rest periods at changeover times.

It is important to coach good technique throughout the practice. It is probably best to 'ban' running straight into a defender as the first attacking option. It is not simply about scoring tries – look for evidence of handling work that has been done previously.

Continuous Touchdown: Running, Handling and Scoring

Equipment: I ball
Grid: 20m
Players: 8
Organization: Four attackers 1, 2, 3, 4, and four defenders in two pairs AB, CD. The attackers start on the centre line, and run, handle and score against the defenders AB. They turn around immediately, beat defenders CD to score, then turn to attack defenders AB again. The coach should keep changing over the attackers and defenders.

Heads Up Rugby and Spotting Spaces in the Defence

However proficient players become at handling, their skills will be of little use if they are not utilized to get the ball to another player in space and/or in a better position on the pitch.

Only a great deal of practice and conditioned games will allow club players to appreciate how to use their passing skills. Sometimes a defender can be 'fixed' from a distance; at other times the attacker has to get in close

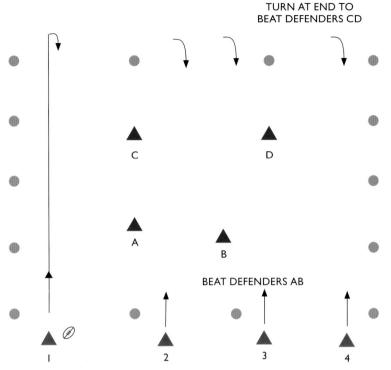

TURN AT END TO
BEAT DEFENDERS CD

C   D

A   B

BEAT DEFENDERS AB

1   2   3   4

Continuous touchdown.

to him before passing. The support player(s) must have some depth, and he should be telling the ball carrier what he wants. The player in support changes with each pass, but the basic principles are the same.

Once these skills are put into a game, there is less time available to the ball carrier and many more bodies enter the equation. Be assured that it is not simple. Your practices will develop the players' skills, but once you get into a game of 'play what you see' with heads-up rugby, the options seem to multiply. With good coaching you may have conditioned some of the players' reflexes to act in a certain way that has good rugby habits, but spotting space requires much practice if the players do not do it automatically.

There are practices that can be used to develop the skill, but your early coaching will

have contained elements of searching and scanning for space and areas that the defenders have not covered.

Breakout

This is a very straightforward practice that can also be fun for the players involved. They might not realize it, but they are using scanning skills and acting quickly when they spot a gap. This is valuable work even in what seems a simple activity, and the coach will soon learn who can see space. It proceeds as follows:

- The ball carriers in the middle run and pass while trying to find a space in the defence (the players in the outside area)

Breakout.

- When the attackers find a space, they have to run through the defended area without being touched
- When the attack starts to score regularly, add to the number of defenders. But if scoring becomes too difficult, redress the balance so that scoring starts again

- The defenders can stand still, but they will quickly realize that they have to work hard to stop the attack scoring at will

Identifying space is a relatively straightforward part in rugby as it is initially an individual skill, but actually getting the ball into that area is

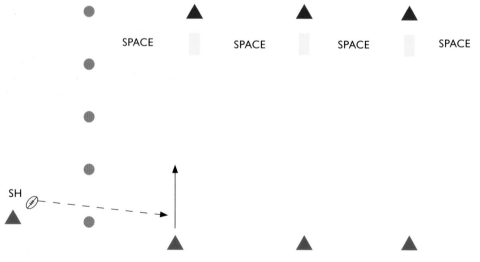

Spotting space.

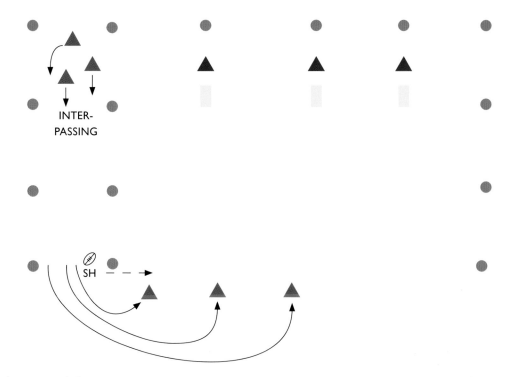

Inter-passing before spotting space.

far more complex than the original identification, and it calls for communication, handling skills and team confidence to play a runner into the space.

This practice soon makes players scan the defence to start identifying when and where spaces emerge.

- Three bags (sausage bags) have a defender behind each
- Three attackers get the ball from a scrum-half pass, and the three defenders step into a space on coach command
- There is always going to be at least one space available (sometimes three if two defenders take the same space), and the attackers must communicate this to the first receiver

As the players improve, the coach can call later and later so that the attackers are given less time to react to what is in front of them.

This can progress by adding three attackers behind the first three, and they come in to support any breakthrough into a free space. This rewards depth in attack, and vital skills are starting to come together; in summary:

- Recognize space
- Communicate that you have seen it
- Play the ball to that space and exploit it
- Add extra runners from depth

When you are concentrating on spotting spaces, the best placed players are usually the deepest or the widest. One of them is likely to spot emerging space better than those with

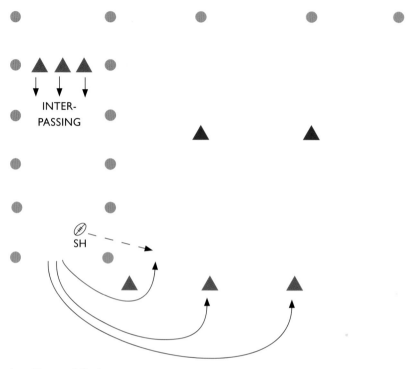

Bags replaced by two defenders.

or close to the ball, so one of those players has to be encouraged to call advice to the players inside or in front of him. When the players are confident with the call, space can be spotted and exploited – especially if the decision-making is carried out quickly and incisively, and the call is accurate and clear.

This practice can be developed further by making the attackers work hard to get to their support position: attackers inter-pass in a narrow channel, run around a cone, and sprint to their position for the same practice as above.

The decision-making can be to hit a free space between or outside the bags, or two defenders can take the place of the bags and the attackers have to get the ball in a space that they leave free.

Spotting *free space to attack* will come quite naturally to some of your players, but others will require coaching assistance. Even the 'natural' individuals will get better with practice, and all players will improve their collective decision-making and reaction to the situation if they are given plenty of opportunity in these sessions.

Starting 'Blind'

In this practice there is no defence in place until the last moment: the coach has his back to the defenders as he faces the attackers. The practice will end up as 5 v 5, but could easily be 4 v 4 until the players improve and understand what they are trying to achieve.

Starting 'blind'.

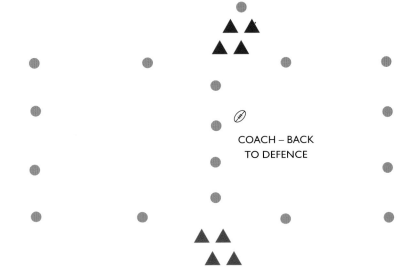

COACH – BACK
TO DEFENCE

- On a call from the coach, the defenders run backwards and round a cone to come back into the practice to defend on either side without any discussion or plan
- Once they come round one side of the end cone, they must stay in that section of the defensive area
- The coach can give instructions on how many he wants on each side, but that should not be necessary as there will always be, at worst, two defenders on each side – three and one, or four and none
- On another call from the coach, the attackers take a pass from the coach, scan the two attacking options, and take the attack to the appropriate side
- The coach can keep changing his call to alter the time available to the attack to make their minds up. If he calls and passes just as the defenders are coming round the cone, little time is available for attacking decision-making. If that call is later, when the defenders are in place, the task becomes easier for the attackers
- The skill being practised is spotting space,

so defence can range from two-handed touch to tackling in tackle suits. The coach must decide on the appropriate level of defence to suit, and challenge the skills of attack and defence
- Once the attack starts, they must play through the defence in front of them – even though they may have gone the 'wrong' way. Players must learn to play through bad decisions and mistakes
- Have a try line so that the attack scores a try at match pace whenever possible
- The coach should watch very carefully for passing technique, lines of running, support, coming on to the ball, attacking the inside shoulder of a defender – all the things that have been coached previously. The correct attacking side decision is merely the start; good team skills are required to score
- The attacking players can start in a huddle so there is no first, second or third player etc., or they can start in Indian file so they have to work hard to take up a support position once the first receiver has decided which side will be attacked

The skill of *scanning* and recognizing weak areas of defence is an advanced skill, but it is worthwhile developing it through practices such as these. Once a mismatch is spotted, the team with the ball needs to attack that area quickly.

Decoy running will always upset defences when the runners look as if they might get the ball. One under-used strategy is to use the blindside winger and encourage him to run for most of each and every game. Both wingers should become the centre of just about all you do in attack – and it is simple in concept. Generally you will see the blindside winger watching the rest of the backs when the ball is spread to the open side – and some wonder why overlaps are hard to create.

The blindside winger must make himself available as a runner at all times, and prob-ably outside your fly half. If the fly half runs an effective holding line to hold in the defend-ing 10 and open side flanker, the defending 12 has a big decision: what to do about the attacking blindside winger. If the defending 12 stays on his own man, the blindside winger can take a short ball from the attacking fly half. However, if the defending 12 comes back to take the attacking blindside winger, a space must appear in the place he has just come from, and a pass from your 10 to your 12 should put your 12 in space.

You may think this is over-simplified, but it will pay dividends, especially if your attacking blindside winger goes late. The tendency is to go too soon so that the defence can see exactly what is happening, and they simply move their own blindside winger to nullify the extra man. If, however, your winger delays until, say, the lineout ball is in the air or the ball is in the scrum, he will be pleasantly surprised at how many opponents switch off and fail to cover his run infield.

Once the blindside winger is working in this manner, the full back can then pose a threat with his incursion, and the defence becomes overloaded as they see more players moving than they are usually accustomed to seeing.

Counter Attack

Counter attack comes very much into this category of effective scanning for spaces, but where and when to go can place enormous decision-making on the first player(s) at the ball. There are two main situations where the decision needs to be made: a kick from the opposition, and the turnover ball.

Players can be helped with advice if they get the ball and are not quite sure what to do next.

Turnover ball: This presents a window of opportunity when the opponents are not

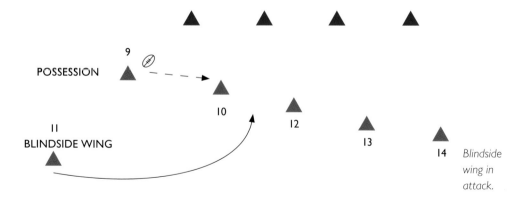

Blindside wing in attack.

organized in defence. The window may be brief, but it does exist.

If there is no defence ahead of the ball at the turnover, the player should pick and go into space and expect his support runners to get to him as quickly as possible.

If the defence has started to reorganize, advise that there should be at least two passes to get outside any organization.

A kick from the opposition: If the opponents kick long and your player feels isolated and unsure of where to go, good general advice can be to *run straight back to where the ball was kicked from and/or to where most of the opposition players are at that moment.* Once

that line is taken, most of the opposition will be held for a while, and the attacking options can be explored outside the original runner.

Poles to Aid Lines of Run Skills

If some players are failing to 'cut' the ball and understand the concept, there is a case for working between poles to assist the learning process.

- The four players stand in Indian file and A1 takes the ball through the first gate
- As he moves forwards the support runners aim for their gate

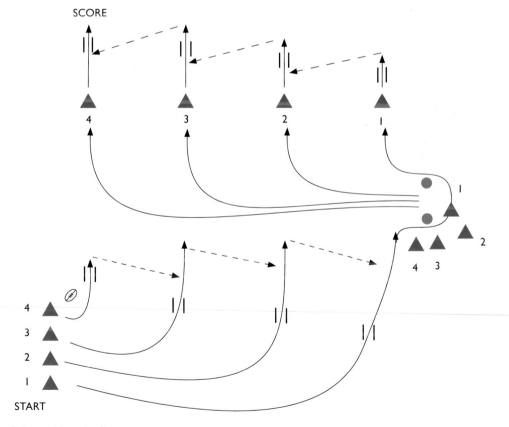

Poles to aid running lines.

- Each pass is made after the attacker goes through his gate
- A4 carries the ball round the two cones and is followed by the others
- A4 takes the ball through the first gate, and the others head for their gate
- The first part of the practice is repeated when passing in a different direction

When the players improve, decrease the distance (length, not width) between the gates, giving the passer less time and space each time.

To hold the first two runners back slightly, ask them to run through their own gate, and then another one before they support.

To stop the practice becoming too predictable, a set of poles can be set up between the cones and you might ask the four to pass a certain number of times in the pole area before getting the ball back to A4, who starts off the second leg. Or there might be tackles against shields, press-ups – anything to minimize predictability.

When the players have completed the handling, always insist on the last man scoring at pace, and if the ball is dropped at any stage, encourage the players to pick up the loose ball and at least try to reorganize and finish the sequence, because this is what would have to happen in a match.

This gives scope for competition against the

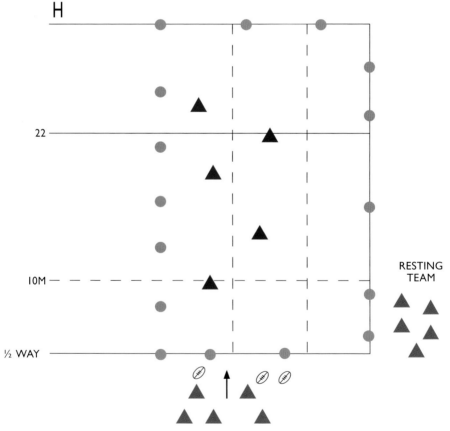

H

22

RESTING TEAM

10M

½ WAY

5 v 5 v 5.

stopwatch and against each other, and there will be a fun element if you can encourage friendly laughter at others' mistakes. Do mix up the teams all the time, and do not let a 'best' team emerge unchanged. However, there is nothing wrong with ending up with a 'select' team to try to beat the existing best time. Remember, though, that you hold the stopwatch and the 'winners' can be anybody you want to win – and there is no rule that states that you have to be totally honest with timekeeping (or what you tell the players regarding the time).

Once a game starts, very little passing is carried out in regular lines where each player has a starting point that he has become used to in skill practices – a useful practice is 5 v 5 v 5 (see the diagram). The players can start with a 'regular' passing movement (all behind the first ball carrier), but it will usually turn into a support practice in which five attack, five defend and five rest. You might have to condition the areas where the defenders must not be active in order to give the attackers a reasonable chance of success, because stopping creativity is much easier than creativity itself.

Always use tackle suits if there is live tackling, and watch very carefully for silly or dangerous tackles. Have three balls at the starting point, and the attackers must sprint back to play another ball after each try. If they fail to score you can accept that, or take the ball back to the start if the mistake was a 'howler'.

There is a fitness element to this practice, and the players always get a rest when they are not directly involved. However, do not let the resting team just rest: they can be placed at each end of the practice and should be encouraged to report back on what they saw. When they become comfortable with this role, the discipline of watching the skills closely should help to improve their own game.

A constant coaching message must be that

players will rarely start where they want to be when a match begins, so it is vital to change people around and/or make them work hard to find an effective line of run.

Once the players have mastered the passing techniques, avoid starting in a straight line of attack. You want the players to spot where they ought to be, and to then work hard to get there. They may know where they will stand from set-piece possession, but much of the game will involve handling from the chaos of tackles, a dropped or kicked ball, and simple errors from both sides. They need to practise the skill of finding their space.

Deception and Evasion

Deception and evasion are easily used terms, but they will require practice for many play-

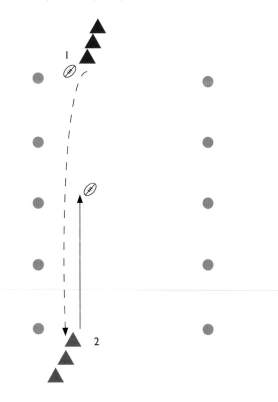

I v I.

ers. Some will be able to lose a defender naturally; others will have to work at it.

This practice can easily be set up so that your whole group is working hard; it is on 1 v 1. This could be used as a warm-up, as a preparation for the main game, or as an individual skill practice at any stage of your session(s), but players of all ages and ability will benefit.

- Player 1 kicks or passes to player 2 (be wary of using a kicking start unless *all* the players have the kicking skills to be accurate most of the time; a long pass is usually the better option)
- Player 2 must run forwards immediately in this practice, and a most important aspect of the game comes into play – to *go forwards*
- 2 takes the pass and tries to beat 1 in the space available
- All sorts of feints and sidesteps, and the use of pace and change of direction will appear; hopefully the players will have many opportunities in a few minutes to give most evasion methods a try
- If 2 is touched or tackled (depending on the rules), he jogs to the end and passes to 3, who kicks or passes to 4 – and the loop continues
- There is no kicking to beat the defender

The practice also prepares the defender for when he has to tackle. The defence in this practice is two-handed touch, but the defender has to learn the most effective ways (*running lines*) to get at the attacker. His *mirroring skills* will be vital in this work, and the coaching message must be to shepherd the attacker to the side where the defender wants him. Conversely, the attacker must work out how to make it as difficult as possible for the defender to achieve this.

There can be a little competition element to this; for example, you can give each player so many attacking chances and find out who scored most times. But a word of warning here: it is likely that the same players will keep getting the best scores, so manipulate your groups so that some of the best attackers have to face each other – and congratulate players who are not so successful but manage to improve.

Raw scores do not always tell the full story, so you must be fully alert to see the player who is really contributing to the practice, and who is making progress. All players of all ages and ability need encouragement: when they get it, they will generally try even harder.

However, the complex game that you are coaching demands that *many skills* are somehow put together to produce just one decent pass – and that is before the really complex stuff begins! To produce that pass, the player in possession has to have got himself into the best position to catch the ball, and must then maintain forward momentum while scanning the pitch for defenders and supporting attackers, drawing/holding an opponent, and giving a pass that attempts to put a support player into forward space.

The simplest starting point for handling skills is to organize 2 v 1 games with two-handed touch below the shoulders as a tackle. You can arrange your squad into groups of three, and mark out an area with cones for each group. If you have too many players to make this practical, arrange them into, say, groups of five or seven, and have one defender defend against waves of attackers – but do remember to keep changing the defender.

It is very important that there are side limits to this practice, and you should not give too much sideways space. Players will quickly develop a lateral running action, and you have to get across the concept of preserving that valuable space. This is a major coaching challenge, yet some players will pick it up straightaway. Others may need guidance, and

'Fixing' a defender then passing.

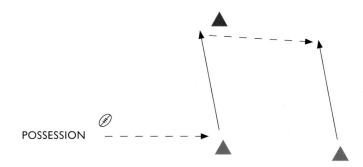

POSSESSION

a useful coaching tip for them from the earliest days is to run at the inside shoulder of the defender to 'fix' him. As there are only two attackers and no primary source of possession, the inside shoulder is a vague concept, so it will help players if the coach places a marker (a bag or cone) at the spot where the possession started.

When coaching, however, you do need to encourage the players to keep running if the defender seems to be standing off to try to cover the second attacker, and this is a skill that will only develop with many practice sessions. You might mention that the ball carrier keeps

an eye on where the defender is placing his weight and/or his line of defence run, but the skill is very much one of awareness rather than 'you must do X when he does Y'. Insist that the ball carrier has made a good decision if he does not pass and manages to score without being touched; this must mean that the defender was marking the support runner and a pass would have led to a tackle and no try.

This 2 v 1 can develop into 3 or 4 v 2, but a note of caution must be added here, in that the skills demanded in 3 v 2 are immensely more complex than in 2 v 1. The numbers

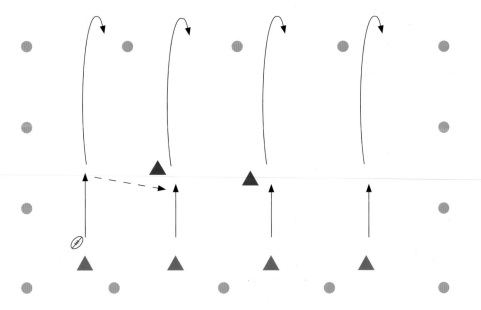

4 v 2.

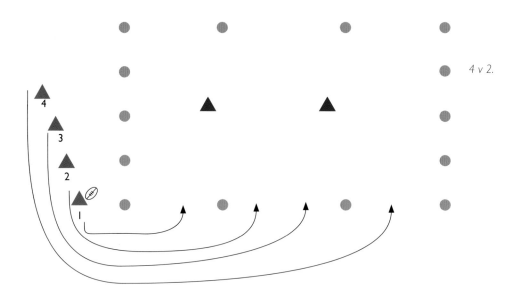

4 v 2.

do not sound significantly greater, but in the reality of playing they are. It may be better to work on 3 v 1 to get a feeling of moving the ball through two passes, but the introduction of two defenders will baffle many players. I would suggest that the more advanced stage from 2 v 1 might be 4 v 2, which can equate into two sets of 2 v 1.

The four attackers come through in waves, and turn round when they score, and try again. This can be timed, and scores compared between groups. If the ball is dropped, just let the attackers pick it up and start again from that point, which will get the valuable message across that you keep playing whatever goes wrong! If there is a knock-on or a player runs off the pitch with the ball, then the team can start again from the back of the pitch.

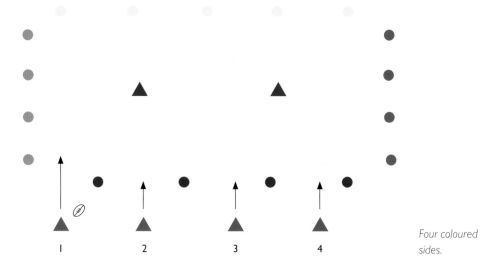

Four coloured sides.

There are all sorts of variations on this theme, and starting from anything other than a flat line will make players work and think.

This will encourage the same handling skills as before, but the attacking players now have to work hard to get to the support position that they want to take up, *and* they have to get on an effective line of run when their instinct probably takes them forwards and sideways away from the pass, when you want them to run forwards and slightly back into the pass. This is the starting point of developing the priceless skill of *cutting the ball*, where the receiver moves slightly into the pass rather than away from it.

A progression on this theme is to cone out a pitch with four different coloured sides, and the attacking three or four players play against two defenders who try to two-hand touch below the shoulder. Once the attackers score at the opposite end from where they started, the scorer calls a colour (but not the one they have just come from), and the attackers run and realign from the ball carrier, who will be the person who scored the last try. This again develops spatial awareness and how to get into an effective line of run/support from an unusual starting position.

Keep stressing the importance of decoy runners, and try to get across that it is not a lazy option. The decoy runner must be in a position to receive a pass or his efforts will be wasted when the defenders know he will not get the ball. Encourage and pick out players who bother to produce the decoy run – it will serve them well in their rugby development.

If the attack struggles, do not hesitate to bring the defence down to one. The whole point of this attacking practice is to develop attacking principles through success; the players do not need the added pressure of continuous failure. And don't be afraid to manipulate proceedings to gain success for these players.

Throughout the coaching process the coach has to invent or choose known activities that challenge his players, whilst the players are given many opportunities to work out the best way to get results. It is probably far better for a player to arrive at his own solution through directed practice and activity, rather than to get there by being told what to do throughout the coaching process. This does put a great load on the coach when drills would be the easy answer, but the good coach will spot when a skill is breaking down, and will reconstruct the practice with sensible modifications to allow the player(s) to progress. This may be as simple as decreasing the number of defenders, or having the defenders run from outside the area to take up their positions so that they, too, are out of the comfort zone. However, the answer may be to increase the size of the playing area and decrease the number of defenders, and this is what good coaching is all about. You have to watch closely to spot what needs to be improved, and you have to practise manipulating the practices/games that are challenging the players.

However the coach structures the session and practice, there are important concepts that should condition what is being worked on:

• Getting width into the attack
• Learning to scan to spot space to attack
• Being aware of how to support the possession your team has
• Using that support to move forwards on to and beyond where you get the ball

Getting width into the attack is not natural, and your players, whatever their age, may find it difficult not to follow the ball. You will need to develop games-based activities to illustrate what width is all about, and coning off two channels at the side of the playing area is simple.

Make your pitch long for this game, and only one attacking player may go in each of the side channels. You can then play a game of touch (see Chapter 4 for the rules), but do referee the defenders carefully and strictly because you want the attack to succeed. The attackers must work to produce a passing movement to get the ball to a player in the side channel or (and this is most important) to break through any weak defence in the middle if the defenders become over-concerned with the attack potential on either side.

Learning to scan to spot space to attack and recognizing it: Remember that the players may not be seeing things the same way that you are. However, the skill of spotting spaces to attack can be encouraged by making the pitch wider, and giving the attack more players and/or decreasing the number of defenders.

The game does need constant revision and discussion to ask the players how they might exploit space, possession and their numerical superiority. But knowing the answers is not the same as producing the answers with the ball, so be prepared to condition how the defenders may defend. Tell them to leave spaces intentionally, and ask them to comply

so that the attacking skills can be encouraged and enhanced. Only by having space to scan can players learn how to scan for that space.

A practice to force players to look closely at what is ahead is 3 v 2 v 2 v 2 (see the diagram below). The middle attacker has three sets of two defenders in front of him, and he has to make a decision each time – does he pass or keep running? And if he decides to pass, to which side?

- A1 runs at the first two defenders
- If he passes, the receiver passes the ball straight back to A1 so that he can run at the second pair of defenders, and so on
- A1 has to 'fix' the defence if he is to pass, then he has to work out which side to pass the ball
- If the defence allows it by trying to cover the support runner(s), he must run straight through them

Developing support play: You need a pitch big enough to allow a game of touch between 5 v 5 with, say, three extra players in different bibs from the other two teams. The object of the game is to score tries, but if the attackers drop the ball, knock on, forward pass or it is intercepted, the floating extra three immediately join the opposition, who are now the attacking team. The signal for the change can come from the coach, and it does not have to follow automatically from a mistake. Have a set call, and when it is shouted, the attacking player must place the ball on the ground, the floating three change sides, and the defenders pick up and attack. You now have a scenario of turnover possession and counter attack, and the players must

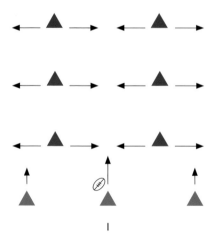

3 v 2 v 2 v 2.

be encouraged to get at the defence before they have time to reorganize.

Using that support to move forwards on to and beyond where you get the ball: To practise this difficult concept, I would suggest the touch game described in Chapter 4. The defence must be refereed to allow realistic attacking opportunities, and the attack may pass only to a player who is running forwards. The coach has to intervene if the safe option is taken to pass to a player who is standing still, and this can lead to a turnover in possession.

Tag Rugby has a useful role to play well beyond the Tag age. It is an easily run game that allows players free rein to attack yet retain possession. The coach needs to encourage players to attack the defenders at pace, as this will allow the defence less time to think, scan and organize.

Of course there will be handling errors, but try to hold on to the theory that it is better to fail a few times than not to attempt something at all. And if the hands are the problem, the coach can always use the whole-part-whole system and concentrate on the aspect(s) of skill that is letting the players down.

All through the game of choice, be it Tag, touch or a conditioned game, players need to be reminded that they should head for an available space if it is directly in front of them, or pass somebody else into such a space or attack the nearest defender's inside shoulder so that the free outside space is maintained.

Sometimes a player will run across the pitch with the ball, which eats into the valuable outside space. Once it happens it cannot be undone, but there are coachable strategies, described earlier, which can be used once the players start to understand what the problem is (lateral running) and how best to straighten it up.

If you manage to achieve some/all of the following in a friendly, structured and fun environment, you will have ticked many coaching boxes:

- Players can catch and pass with *two hands on the ball*
- Attacking players are aware of their role in working hard to offer the ball carrier *various passing options*
- Attacking players are comfortable in trying to beat opponents with *evasion and deception*
- Defenders work hard to *close down* the space options the attacking team are trying to develop
- *Teamwork* is vital in both attack and defence
- *Changes of direction, running at space, and pace and length of pass* can beat well organized defence
- Constructive communication is vital in attack and defence, even (especially!) at the formative stages of coaching
- The *players have a say* in the way the coaching is structured
- The *players improve* and have a better idea of the rudiments of the game at the end than they ever did at the start
- The *players want more!*
- The *coach wants more!*

CHAPTER 7

INTRODUCING RUGBY WITH CONTACT

The Tackle

The tackle will come naturally to many players, but the coach at all levels must be aware that some players will not enjoy it. Once some introductory work has been done on elementary contact, the tackle will have been greatly assisted by Tag rugby, where the defenders got used to placing themselves in a good pre-tackling position by sprinting and reaching to try to get the tags from an attacker.

Tackling has some key coaching aspects that are often overlooked:

- The tackler must keep his eyes open to see the target of the opponent's upper thigh at all times
- A tackler should not dive into a tackle. He should run as far as possible and tackle the ball carrier without leaving a space that requires a dive

- He should keep moving through the tackle (drive) and make contact with the appropriate shoulder and not the arm. An arm tackle is weak and invites injury
- Once the shoulder makes contact the head should be *behind* the tackled player
- The tackler should drive from the legs, keep his head slightly up and look at a point beyond the tackle. This action should keep his back straight (spine in line)
- As soon as the ball carrier hits the ground, the tackler should be coached to stand up and try to lift the tackled ball so that he has tackled *and* got possession for his team

Early development into the tackle might require different amounts of time with different players. Early tackles might be best working in pairs, with both players in a kneeling position, and the tackle is made as one player starts to get up to run away.

The next stage might be to execute a tackle as the ball carrier jogs slowly past a kneeling player, who makes the tackle.

If the tackle is practised from no more than a jog, ensure that a jog is as fast as it becomes. Then stress that the tackler should move into the tackle without diving, because when he dives he has no control and is

Both players kneel pre-tackle.

Tackle from kneeling as the player moves away.

effectively out of the game. It is likely, though, that your 'weak' tackler will develop better in conditioned games than in 'cold' practice.

Tackling is an odd part of rugby. Some players love the physicality of the encounter, while others will never be comfortable with it. The coach should not worry too much about the player who does not enjoy tackling, because there are many of them who are fast enough to make some sort of an attempt at a 'scrag' tackle on the opponent's upper body and/or shirt in preference to going around his legs. That same player might just be your speed merchant who can score more points than he gives away, so accept that you will not get every player in the group to tackle classically around the legs. It is just one single skill in a wide range of them in rugby.

A very important coaching lesson for all players is to understand what they may do at a tackle; this is best coached from the outset. The tackler may stand up immediately after the tackle (and the tackled player is on the ground) and then play the ball; the tackled player may release and leave the ball on the ground, stand up, and then play the ball. This is easier for the tackler than the tackled player and can be coached from the early days.

The tackler should get to his feet, straddle the tackled player and *lift* the ball. Again, the strong body shape is used so that he is strong and prepared for any later contact.

If neither player can get up, the third player (the first to the tackle) may play the ball and lift it away from the contact area as there is no ruck with just the tackler and the tackled player on the ground. The key coaching point is that the lifting action should be the first option to the third player if it is available.

The coach can help all players in practice by telling them when the tackle ball may be lifted. As long as they 'come through the gate' they are onside. 'The gate' is not a complex concept, and all players need to be coached

The gate.

In from the side of the gate.

Half squat.

A template for ruck, maul, tackle and scrum.

strongest body shape can be seen in weight-lifting.

Turn that basic shape forwards 45 degrees and you have a template for ruck, maul, tackle and scrum. Some call the shape 'spine in line', and this is a good coaching instruction, but there also needs to be a drop into a strong shape where the legs provide the forward momentum and the head is slightly tilted up to straighten the spine; with the head down, the spine tends to assume a weak convex shape.

Contact practices on tackle shields need to be handled carefully, as bad habits do creep in easily. Always check the shield holders to make sure they do not hold the straps in one hand, which can easily lead to an injury when the tackle comes in. Ensure that both grips are held.

Work in short distances as you do not want the tackler running too far into contact; the aim should be to use the shields to develop

into using it at all entries into the tackle area, ruck and maul in each and every practice session.

It does mean that they have to be aware of the law, and then adjust their line of run so that they come in from behind the ball and not from the side.

There is one common theme (yet again!) that needs to be understood once contact comes into a game, be it in a match or in practice: the body needs to be in an effective shape for the contact, and the best and

Potentially dangerous shield grip.

LEFT: Safe shield grip.

BELOW: Kneeling pre-contact.

power, not the speed of the run. The best starting position is from kneeling or from the floor.

This takes the pace out of the contact, which would probably have had one of two outcomes if it had been carried out too quickly: the impetus would have been transferred upwards, or the shield holder would have been knocked over. Make sure players practise with alternate shoulders so that they do not favour one side over the other when they employ their 'favourite' shoulder.

However much you practise handling skills, your players will be tackled at some time in every game. However well they pass and/ or beat a defender, there will sometimes be a need for contact skills so that the best option is taken at the tackle or immediately after it.

At all times coach evasion rather than collision, but do coach what happens next when the evasion has not worked. A well timed pass (pass just before contact) close to a would-be tackler can keep the ball alive and allow a better placed support runner the opportunity to advance. That will not always

Lying prone pre-contact.

be possible, however, and various scenarios emerge:

- Offload during the tackle
- The mini maul: held up but not tackled to the ground
- Tackled to the ground, but can get a pass in from the back-down position
- Held up and the ball cannot be offloaded
- Tackled to the ground

There is no doubt that crashing into contact and forming a ruck or maul is easiest to coach, and many players enjoy the easy option where no real decision is considered. Unless the coach asks for more, players will see contact as the simplest available choice. But the offload should be an aim for players of all levels and ages. It is a real game breaker, and successful offloading makes the game more fluid and dynamic.

Offload.

The Offload

One of the best starting points for the offload skill is to introduce it into a game of controlled touch. Play a game and explain to the players that the coach will call 'held' at various times in that game. As soon as he calls it, the player with the ball has to run towards a defender, slow down, and the defender wraps his arms around the ball carrier's waist. The ball carrier tries to get the ball around the defender's back, then plays the ball from behind the defender to a support player before he hits the ground.

There are some very important coaching points in this process:

- The ball must not be 'passed' at a support runner: it should be *lifted* behind the defender so that the support runner can choose how to take the lifted

'Wrong' side offload.

pass. If the ball is passed, the player in contact has determined where the support runner will take the pass when a hanging pass is better to judge for the incoming player

- If the ball carrier is not comfortable with the offload, he should not carry on with the pass. If he is not in full control of the ball or the support is not in place, it is far better to take the tackle and play for a ruck or maul
- The support must come from depth as it is very easy to overrun the offload pass
- If the support player gets too flat he will probably overshoot the pass because the contact, adjustment of the ball and a lifted pass take a while. Players will appreciate the need for depth if the coach gives plenty of opportunities for the offload in this game of touch
- Players should be encouraged to use left and right offload passes so they do not become proficient on one side only
- The pass will usually be given behind the defender, but coaches should be aware that it may be given on the side that the player goes in on the defender. The support might be on that side and a player giving the pass might be able to play the ball there. A successful offload on the 'wrong' side is preferable to losing it on the 'correct' side

After players become comfortable with the offload in touch games, the skill can be practised in narrow grids with defenders. The process is exactly the same as in the game of touch, with small groups running through a group of tacklers in tackle suits in a narrow area. This is not a tackling practice, and all that is needed is a tackle that slides around

the player and allows him to fall to the ground behind the tackle.

At all stages the player in possession should allow himself to hit the floor behind the tackler. The offload pass can be given at any stage between contact and the body going to ground.

It is best to coach players to hold the ball in two hands throughout the execution of the offload. The players might feel that the one-handed pass could be the easier option: it can be, but it can go easily wrong when the ball is behind the tackler's back, and it can be knocked out of a one-hand grip by another defender behind the tackle. If the ball is in two hands it is less likely to be dislodged by any defender or by the tackle itself.

You may come across a player who can perform the skill one-handed. Let him do just that, but coach him in the two-handed method because he may need it at some point; and let the other players know that

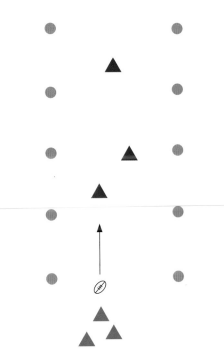

Offload in narrow channel.

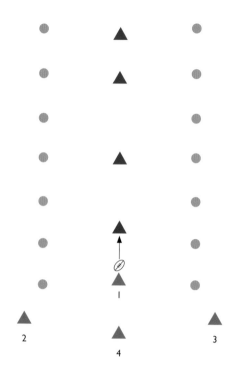

Offload.

- The attack of four faces the defence in a diamond formation. The two outside runners must stay outside their touch-line until a tackle is made. There will be a tendency for them to creep closer to the action, but the coach must remind them that they stay outside the line until the tackle starts
- The lead player A1 takes the ball into the first tackle, and the player who is taking the offload pass must let his partners know this
- If A2 or A3 takes the offload pass, that player becomes A1 in the next offload
- A4 moves up into the wing position, and A1 gets off the floor to become A4
- If the tackled player cannot offload to A2 or A3, he passes (from the ground and on his back) to A4, who then becomes A1 while the other two scramble to the two side positions as A2 and A3, and the player on the floor fills in as A4

he is a special case with this skill, while most others require two hands.

With plenty of opportunity to practise the offload skill, players might understand another vital rugby skill: when not to go through with it. There are times when the player will be held up and cannot pass the ball on safely.

When they can produce the skill on a regular basis, there is an offloading practice that demands the offload, then reorganization, and a great deal of communication:

- The channel width should be between the 5m line and the 15m line

The practice does illustrate the fact that offloading opportunities can be spotted from

Too high at contact.

Low into contact.

Lead with the elbow to secure the ball at contact.

a considerable width/distance from the ball carrier.

The Mini Maul: Held Up but not Tackled to the Ground

The earliest contact will be the maul, and it can be introduced at an early stage. Once a player is held up or tackled, contact knowledge, awareness and relevant skills become important.

The first important aspect of this contact when a player is held up and does not go to ground concerns the ball carrier, who needs to be aware that his is a crucial role because he sets the height of the ball for the support runner, who will latch on to it. If he holds the ball too high, the support player's impetus is dissipated into the air with a weak entry.

However, if the ball carrier works hard to hold the ball lower, the man coming in will be forced to adopt a much stronger and more dynamic entry on to the ball.

Next comes the method of latching on to the ball. The strongest and safest way to coach this is not to use the fingers at the start of the process: the player coming on to the ball should lead in with his elbow and shoulder before he does anything else.

The support player needs to be encouraged to make an early decision on going on to the ball. Many players see the contact situation, then run towards it and fall on to the ball. However, this is a weak position, and it can be coached to become better and more dynamic.

Ask the players to drop into a low-backed and low-legged position for a few paces, with their eyes concentrating on the ball before they try to take it. The low run does not come naturally, but persistence in its use will pay dividends.

Players do have various available options with the ball 'up': they can:

- Drive forwards as a pair
- Twist the ball out and run forwards
- Twist the ball out and feed another runner

Possession that is won with what is effectively a mini-maul can be the fastest available from any contact situation – far quicker than a ball won at a ruck, for instance. Coaches often worry about how the first support player should win the ball. Ideally he will enter with shoulder and elbow with his strongest side. If the man being held has the ball on the right side of the support, that ball winner should go in with his right shoulder/elbow

If the ball is on his left, the left shoulder/elbow should lead. However, as in all coaching, it can be a case of 'needs must'. There is a stronger side in most situations, but it is far better to win possession with the 'wrong' shoulder leading than not to win it at all.

The mini-maul can be introduced as a first introduction to contact at the tackle area. The simplest way to practise it is to have groups of three players. The ball carrier jogs (no faster), then stops at an imaginary tackle and presents the ball. The second player jogs in low, hits the ball, and twists it (in one movement if possible) to the third player. He then jogs, imagines he is held, presents the ball, and the other two players talk to let each other know who is carrying out which role.

The next stage would be to introduce another player holding a tackle shield. His role is not to hit anybody with the shield: he is there simply to hold up the forward momentum and to offer sensible resistance so the practice becomes more realistic.

A mini-maul ingredient can be introduced into a game of touch. At times the coach will call out 'Held', and the ball carrier on the call must slow down and allow himself to be wrapped up (but not tackled to the ground) by the immediate defender. The next available player on the attacking team has to run in low and twist the ball out to a support runner. The game of touch carries on as usual until the next call of 'Held'.

One weakness in the process can easily be when the first support player 'drops' on to the ball because he reacts only when he gets to the tackle area. He must be coached to start to drop to contact height *well before* he gets to the ball. Once he does that and the ball carrier works to get the ball to an effective height, the possession has a better chance of being won in a dynamic method.

Watch closely for the ball carrier, who turns his back to the opponents. He is very much out of the game, though sometimes he can do little about his situation because of what the defenders have done. If possible he should go into contact with a shoulder and carry the ball slightly behind. He should not lead with the ball into the defender as it is so easy to lose the ball in that position.

If possible he should drop the body slightly at the knees so that he is not straight-legged because he can offer little in that weak, perpendicular position.

This mini-maul can, at a later stage of player development, be the basis of a full driving maul, and the best habits of body height and ball presentation ought to be coached early.

Some players will be able to trail the ball in one hand, which does keep it away from the defenders. However, it can easily be spilled from this type of carry, so players should be coached to keep both hands on the ball if they cannot manage a safe hold with one hand.

Ball up left.

Backing into contact.

The player coming in on the ball should drive through it, and his effort and momentum should not end as he touches the ball. He may go forwards a mere couple of centimetres, but coaching that will reinforce the need to head forwards whenever possible.

However, there are situations when the

game has lost momentum and the support player's only option is to win and recycle the ball. Even then he should be coached to 'hit' the ball so there is a degree of dynamism in the situation.

Too high at contact.

Tackled to the Ground but not Held

If the player with the ball is forced to the ground, there is a brief window of opportunity to play the ball two-handed to a support player. The ball should be pushed upwards if a runner is available, but if the tackler is still holding the ball carrier, he will have to perform the pass quickly or a penalty kick will be awarded for playing the ball after a tackle.

The more skilled players will cope with the decision making in this pass, but it should be available to all. The key is for the support runner to call if it is 'on', as the player on the ground will not see what is around him.

Strong contact position.

Trailing the ball one-handed at contact.

Trailing the ball two-handed at contact.

Tackled to the Ground and a Ruck Develops

Early ruck work can be started in a game of touch. When the coach calls 'Tackle', the ball carrier slows, goes to the ground and places the ball behind his body. The next two attackers bind as they run to the ball, put one foot beyond it and the possession continues in the game of touch till the next call of 'Tackle' from the coach.

This can develop with the use of tackle shields. Have a few defenders holding shields and one of them moves to the 'Tackle', stands over the ball and is rucked by the two players who have created a bind.

A key element in the ruck is that players must be encouraged to slow down before the contact: it should never be at flat-out pace or the players will easily fall over instead of rucking. They must bring their backsides close

together as they bind, drop their body height, and try to get into the most effective position for contact. This bind, bringing the backsides together, is important because if they do not get close, one can easily be split from his partner if support comes in and pushes him outwards instead of forwards.

In both ruck and maul the coach needs to stress the coaching point that the time *before* the contact will have a major part in determining the outcome. The ball carrier will send out important information as he goes into contact, and the support players must practise to recognize it.

For example, the ball carrier will start to lead with one shoulder when he is aware that he has to make contact. The support player can learn to recognize the direction of turn as soon as it starts, which is often a distance away from the eventual contact area. He should start to drop into an effective body position as soon as he is aware that he will be needed – not after the contact occurs. This can save vital time, even though it may be just a split second, and encourages players to scan for information from an early age.

All early work in building up to any ruck contact must be precise. The first requirement is for the ball carrier to present a static target (the ball) for the support players. Many players will not immedi-

Two bind over the ball.

Two-hand plant.

ately take to this part of the game, and sensible, sympathetic coaching is required.

The ball carrier has to be comfortable with hitting the ground *and* placing the ball. The first major coaching task is to coach the tackled player to hit the ground *before* there is any attempt to place the ball; this should be carried out with both hands on the ball.

There may be some players who can 'plant' the ball with one hand, but it can be less than safe when there are other players around, the ball is wet, and the carrier starts the planting action slightly before his body is static. It is important to coach techniques that will work time and time again.

The early ruck work can be done without a ball carrier, and the carried ball can be introduced later in the process when the ruck techniques are becoming clearer to the players.

1. Work in pairs with one holding a tackle shield. The working player stands no more than two paces away, drops into a low driving position, and moves the shield backwards no more than two paces. The shield holder must not try to knock his partner back: he is offering sensible resistance, and that will require early instruction on what is acceptable and especially

One-hand plant.

what is not acceptable. Do not wait until there is a problem before laying down the ground rules on the use of the shield.

2. The working player places one hand on a ball, then makes contact with the shield, as in 1, and drives forwards for two to three paces. He must not knock the shield holder off his feet: it is his responsibility to hold him upright if there is any possibility of that happening.
3. A ball is placed just in front of the shield and the working player steps over the ball, then makes contact with the shield, as in 1.
4. Now work in pairs against the shield. Place a ball in front of the shield (as in 3).

Touch the ball before contact.

Two players bind at the waist so that their hips and shoulders touch. They step over the ball (both stepping forward with the outside foot is best), use their outside arm to grasp the shield holder, and take the shield back two paces without making any contact with the ball.

5. This introductory work to the ruck can move to three players against one tackle shield when the coach is satisfied with the standard of the previous work.

Drive into contact after touching the ball.

This practice introduces a ball carrier, who steps into the shield and drives it slightly backwards before going to ground. He falls with his back to the shield and his body straight across the pitch so that the support players can step over him with relative ease and safety. Once he makes contact with the ground (and not before) he places the ball at arm's length so that it stays still and does not move around:

- The shield holder then steps back slightly so that he is just behind the player on the ground

Two players drive into the shield at contact.

- The two support players bind (as in 4), and drive over and beyond the man on the floor, then against the resistance of the shield for two to three paces whilst avoiding the ball and stepping over the player on the ground (who should cover his head with his hands after placing the ball – but not before or during that process)

6. This stage does not need to be rushed. Ensure that good technique is carried out at all times, the players know what they are trying to achieve, and the techniques have been emphasized and carried out in all the introductory progressive work. Then the process can become more fluid as the almost static nature of the introductory phases needs to be given realistic movement.

    This stage becomes 4 v 2 v 2. The start is the same as in the previous practice (5), then continues along the following lines:

    - As the first two players make contact with the shield, a second defender steps forwards to assist the shield holder in resisting the drive of the two attackers. The coach must emphasize that 'resistance' is adequate and this player is not there to try to win any confrontation in the contact
    - As soon as the two attackers hit the shield, the third attacker steps in to bind between the two who are driving against the shield. All three hold their forward momentum (not easy and needs constant practice), then drive forwards to step over and clear the ball
    - The fourth attacker picks up the ball, takes it forwards, and restarts the same process against the second pair of defenders. He must not rush

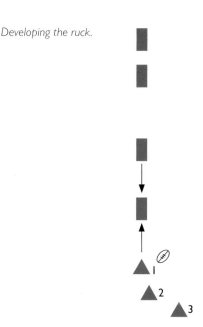

Developing the ruck.

the process, and needs to slow until the support is ready (that is, off the ground)

This process can carry on ad infinitum with the 'used' defenders jogging back to present a new target. This, however, needs to be handled very carefully as the exercise is there to develop correct technique; it is not a coach's tool to tire out the players.

Do not ask too much from tired bodies, as this type of work can become very demanding very quickly. Keep changing players' roles so that boredom can be avoided, and always stress what good technique is: it will soon disintegrate when the players have not got the strength to reproduce the skill, and low running and contact will sap their strength and stamina.

Your practice development must enable the players to become comfortable with hitting the ground, and to feel safe while the players above them know their role and carry it out with precision at all times.

Once the coach is confident in the players' ability to reproduce the skills in the mini-ruck, little games can be invented to make things more game-related. For example, place five or six defenders in a space no wider than 5m, with four attackers facing them. The defenders must accept that they cannot take any further part in the game once they have been 'rucked' and they must immediately leave the 5m channel so that it becomes uncluttered.

The attackers also need the rules of the game to be explained carefully, as you are now asking them to take contact when previously you have stressed evasion. The contact here is a means to an end – live ruck practice.

The attackers have to make contact with any shield in front of them and use the skills

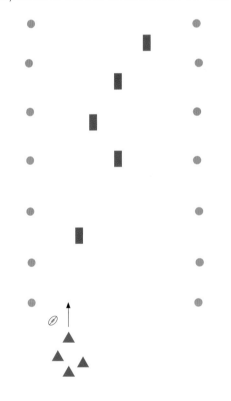

Live ruck practice.

from the previous development work to keep the possession moving through all the shields to the end of the channel.

This sequence will be difficult to accomplish and it will be tiring, so give plenty of recovery time and stay vigilant to ensure that the players are carrying out what has been coached in the build-up work.

Once the players can succeed with a length, double the workload by getting them to turn round at the end and come back in the opposite direction. There will inevitably be mistakes, so do praise achievement even when it may only be partial success.

Where the ball is placed on the ground becomes important when live opposition plays and they are trying to get the ball:

- The best possession will probably come from a ball held back and placed at arms' length with both hands. That is a long (and unstable) distance for a defender to stretch across to try to get possession
- But there will be occasions – usually bodies in the way of where the player wants to place the ball – when the ball has to be held and placed close to the body. This becomes easier for the defenders to try to lift the ball as they are relatively strong and they do not have to lean across
- At some stage there will be a need to roll the ball backwards because the opposition can win the possession. This should be called by the next player (often the scrum-half), who recognizes that the retention of possession is not assured and a different skill is required. The essential ingredient is control of the roll. The ball must not be thrown back, but rather placed with both hands and then (and only then) rolled backwards to a waiting player in close proximity who should have called for the ball to be rolled

Two hands placing the ball backwards at the tackle.

Unstable defender when the ball is well back.

Defender is stronger when the ball is closer to the tackle.

CHAPTER 8

THE SCRUM

The scrum has to be viewed as a dependable source of quality possession at all levels of the game. There tends to be an aura around the skills involved, and some coaches feel less than confident in coaching it. However, there are certain basic principles to the scrum, and once they are understood, the area of primary possession is not so very complex.

The earliest work with young players must involve their being aware of what constitutes a *strong, stable, athletic position* from which they can start a scrum. This early work is best done with all players, just as you would practise handling and evasion with everybody.

The following warm-up exercise will soon highlight what a strong athletic position can do – and what happens in its absence.

Split the group into pairs, who face each other. Get them to hold their partner's right wrist in their left hand, then ask them to try to touch their partner's left ear with their index finger while stopping their partner from doing the same to them.

This work will soon show which players

Hold the wrists.

Ball balanced on the back.

lose their balance too quickly – and nearly always it is because they are too straight-legged and not stable. The position of the feet can be a useful coaching starting point:

- Feet just wider than shoulder width
- Knees slightly bent
- Weight spread evenly over both feet
- Weight on the front of the foot – do not sit back on the heels
- Face forwards with the whole body, which should be square-on to the target area

The scrummage position must be shown early in the process, and *shoulders above the hips* can be felt by the players as they kneel in the press-up position with knees apart, hands below the shoulders, and head slightly up with the chin off the chest. Working in pairs, get one player to balance a ball on the small of the other player's back – if the ball rolls off, readjustments need to be made:

- If it rolls forwards – the hips are too high or the back is arched
- If it rolls off backwards – the back and legs are too straight or the hips are too low
- If it rolls off sideways – the hips are twisted

Binding

Binding is next in the process. Players should work in groups of three, and practise binding with all three facing forwards with their backs in line with the touchline – spines in line.

Front row bind.

THE SCRUM

Spines in line.

Kneeling three-man scrum.

Tight-head prop takes the outside bind.

Getting young players into a safe engagement may require some confidence building; the hooker especially will feel vulnerable when his hands are both engaged. Engagement while kneeling will help, and the coach should now start to get players used to the referee's commands of 'Crouch. Bind. Set.'

The next stage will be a three-man scrum from standing. The following are the key points to stress:

CROUCH. BIND. SET.

A scrum engagement global trial was introduced by the IRB (International Rugby Board) for the 2013/2014 season and it was to be played at all levels. The former command of 'Crouch – Touch – Set' was replaced by 'Crouch – Bind – Set.'

- As soon as the three come together, they should bind and check that their feet are pointing forwards, and that they are in a stance with the feet slightly wider than shoulder width
- On 'Crouch', all three bend at the hips, knees and ankles while looking slightly ahead and through the eyebrows, with the chin slightly off the chest and the back firmly set
- On 'Bind', the two front rows should be close enough together that the props can easily bind in accordance with the law.
- On 'Set' they all put their head to the left of their opposite number, with the tight-head prop (on the right) taking the outside bind. There should be no binding on the elbow and the scrum should be square, stable and parallel with the touch line.

The 'Touch' phase is not now part of the scrum

Locks to the side before binding.

Locks turn in to bind.

Props' feet.

Props' feet (after rotation).

engagement global trial, but it can still be used by the coach in the early days to get young players comfortable. There is absolutely nothing wrong with a 'touch' slightly before the 'bind' in practice sessions with learners so that they gain in confidence.

The referee (or coach) tells the scrum-half to put the ball in with, 'Yes 9.'

Let young players experiment with this many times so that they become comfortable with the procedure and change positions around so that they learn what it feels like in different positions.

The Second Row

When the five-man scrum begins, the important factor is binding between the two second-row players.

Begin by forming the front row, and have the two second-row players stand to the outside of the prop they will be binding on, and grip the waistband of their prop just above the pocket (or where a pocket would be).

They then crouch and swing slowly round to engage between the hips of the prop and hooker, making sure that they aim for the gap between the two players' knees.

A bind is made between the second row as they slowly meet and engage.

They work their head up to place their shoulder beneath the buttock of the prop they are engaging on.

One problem that can emerge at all levels and age groups is that it can be difficult for the locks to get their head into the scrum when the front row players are binding tightly. the props need to maintain their bind, however, so do not suggest that they move away from each other to allow the lock to enter. Instead, try the following:

- The prop (or both props if necessary) swivels his inside foot with the heel going slightly away from the hooker
- This means that the tight-head prop (right) swivels his left foot in an anti-clockwise direction

- The loose-head prop (left) swivels his right foot in a clockwise direction
- The distance that the foot moves is not much, but it can free up a slight gap that allows the second row to get in without losing any binding stability in the front row. If this goes wrong, the effects will spread and will probably lead to an ineffective scrum bind and, therefore, an ineffective scrum.

All five players should be comfortable and fully aware of the following checklist:

- Weight slightly on the front of the feet, not on the heels
- Feet slightly wider than shoulder width
- Knees slightly bent
- The weight is spread evenly over both feet
- All the front of the body is facing forwards
- The shoulders are above the hips when crouching

No. 8 bind.

Right flanker's bind.

Left flanker's bind.

- The players look slightly ahead and through the eyebrows with the chin off the chest

The back row can now come into the scrum with a relatively straightforward bind.

These basics ought to provide a sound template of technique for young players as they progress through the game and its age groups. The weightlifting shape should be in players' minds all through their career.

Building Up the Scrum

There is a tendency to practise as eight when

One player on the machine.

Straight legs at the scrum.

players become older, but it is well worth building up the scrum from individual work, then to put it together when the players better understand individual roles and techniques.

It is also worth practising strong technique individually on a scrum machine before putting the front row together. Make sure that the machine is set at the right height for the size of the players to show the best position, and allow some 'give' in the heads by taking some springs off. The coach needs to test the amount of 'give' before putting any player into contact, or to ask some of the better players to feel the 'give' by starting softly and gradually increasing the power that goes into the machine's head.

Once individual contact is made it is important to coach players to maintain their strong back position. Their head position should be slightly up so that they keep looking just ahead, rather than down. However, there should not be too much upward tilt of the head as this can be potentially dangerous if the entry to the scrum is wrong, and a front-row player's head makes accidental contact with his opposite number instead of a gap. Do encourage the use of the eyes to look ahead, as this is far safer than lifting the head too far above the back's horizontal plane (look through the eyebrows).

Keep the scrum forces minimal in the early stages. All players, young or old, need to get a feel for the memory of what good technique feels like. This technique is all-important, so it is good to spend time on this facet of the game well before the season begins.

There are two tips that the coach can give to all players in this individuals scrummaging practice:

- Shorten the length of the neck by trying to bring the head slightly back into the body
- Suck in the abdominals and tighten them just before the scrum begins, and try to hold them in throughout the scrum

1 v 1 scrum position.

Short bind for loose-head prop.

Long bind for loose-head prop.

Do look for the basic shape of the half squat being maintained at the scrum. Players tend to get into a straight-legged position, which is weak and ineffective. If the machine's head has too much 'give', coach the players to 'chase' the contact so that they shuffle their feet forwards to maintain the strong half-squat position.

This may seem unnecessary at this early stage when there is no real pressure in the scrum, but good technique will serve the players well later in their development, and the emphasis on doing things correctly is a very useful coaching tool. It also gets a picture of good technique into their minds at an early stage in their development.

This process might require time and patience because the players may not push, and for many it is a difficult position to hold. You might carry out I v I conditioning to get them used to the position before putting them on the scrum machine or into live 3 v 3 scrums.

The tendency can be for the scrum to collapse, though the IRB scrum engagement trial should have improved this area, so binding and sound body positions are crucial. Some players will not be comfortable initially with putting their head into the gap, so do not assume that it is a simple process, but spend time on it.

One technique that is vitally important is for the loose-head prop to start with a firm bind. This can be most important in minimiz-

Power bind for locks.

ing the danger of a collapsed scrum. He has two options, both very strong: the short arm bind, and the long arm bind.

Front Row in the Scrum

Practise with a front row going down together into the machine. They will tend to concentrate on a new facet and may forget the techniques of the individual work – but keep reminding them of these techniques!

At this stage the coach should call them in with the referee's calls of

- 'Crouch.'
- 'Bind.' A bind is made on the scrum machine handles or on the opponents
- 'Set.' The front rows then engage after a short phase when they are stationary

Have your scrum-half available to put the ball in so that he and the hooker get used to what each needs. Try to encourage possession where the ball moves backwards without any sticking points from hooker to when it emerges from the scrum.

Front Five

When the scrum goes to five players, the back two should be doing the same sort of preparation as the front three. Their body shape is exactly the same, the feet are shoulder-width apart, and they should have their weight on the front studs. Their bind should be strong without going too far around the other player's body.

There are two ways for the locks to start before binding on to the front row: bind and kneel, then go on to the front row in the scrum engagement; or bind and crouch without putting the knees on the floor.

The entry from kneeling is less tiring, but it can allow (or even encourage) an upward movement into the engagement and the power is lost upwards. The crouch position does place stress on players' legs, but it may end with a better engagement. A useful tip can be to ask the forwards, especially the locks, to imagine that they are on the edge of a swimming pool and ready to start a race. If they are too comfortable they are probably not ready for a productive scrum engagement.

The five-man scrum can be practised on the scrum machine, and it is at this stage that best technique should become the norm.

The scrum-half should be available again to put the ball in. One major coaching point at the introduction of scrums is 9 → 2 → 9 (scrum-half → hooker → scrum-half) possession that flows in one seamless movement from the scrum-half put-in, to a hooker's deflection to the scrum-half who has run behind the scrum and can take a moving ball. It is worth practising this so that the ball does not get trapped in any scrum, be it three-man, five-man or eight-man. If the movement has to be stunned at the back because it may be travelling too quickly, that can be easily done; but a stuck, motionless ball in the middle of a scrum is very difficult to get moving again.

Once the eight-man scrum is allowed, a power bind may suit best. The locks bind between the legs of their prop.

CHAPTER 9

THE LINE-OUT

The most important skill in any line-out is the throw. You can have the best jumper in the world, but without an accurate throw his efforts and skills will be largely wasted.

You need to find a group of players who can perform the torpedo throw, then work on their technique. This throw is just like the quarterback pass in gridiron. For rugby purposes, two hands should be on the ball, with the non-throwing hand supporting and stabilizing the ball.

An important part of the throw is the use of the knees. They initiate the movement of the upper body in a style similar to the basket-ball free shot. Knees start, then arms flow in afterwards. It does not have to be a big knee dip – just enough to start the ball movement.

Both hands come up together, but the non-throwing arm is just there to steady the ball before release.

The jumper must be coached into a dynamic jumping style if it does not happen naturally. The starting position should be just above a half squat, and the arms should be down so that they can be driven upwards to assist vertical propulsion. A jump without the arms coming in will be very low.

All players, and certainly the ones who might be receivers, should look as if the ball is coming to them. Do not end up with one lone player looking as if he will get the ball: the defenders pick that up very quickly and know where to place their best jumper.

Once you have the line-out organized, the catcher must use both hands (fingers in the 'W' position again) and be aware that the possession is all too easily wasted if he transfers the ball loosely. If he slaps the ball it is difficult for the scrum half to take. If he wants to pass to the scrum half when

Grip for the throw-in at the line-out.

he is off the ground, there should be a brief moment between catching and pushing the ball (stun and push). This adds control to what might become a loose piece of possession.

The jumper should practise putting his inside arm up first so that he is just slightly sideways on to the ball. However, he does not want his whole back to be showing to the opponents during the jumping phase. Once he has the ball the slight rotational impetus will turn him so that he can end up with his back to the opponents.

If you have no decent jumper, movement from the potential jumpers is all you can practise. Try to get one player (at least) into a space and get the throw in quickly. However, do not limit your jumpers to forwards: you may well have a back who has the best vertical jump; if that is so, use him. It is better to win possession with one player out of position

than to lose it with everybody in the 'correct' place. The same goes for throwing in: it does not have to be a hooker. Pick the player best suited to the skill.

The Lift

Once the lift comes into the game, whatever you come up with, do not allow lifting on the shorts. Not only can this be extremely painful for the man being lifted, but it is also a very poor lifting method, as much of the dynamic of the lift is lost as the fabric of the shorts moves.

The correct grip is shown in the photograph on page 132, and the main coaching point after that is that the two lifters should move together so that they are almost touching. This ensures that each lifter is working through a strong, vertical back (good weight-lifting technique) and not through the arms

Lift on shorts.

Effective lift.

alone, which is a very weak lifting position and tires the lifters' arms out extremely quickly.

One aspect of line-out play that does not get enough practice time is the opposition mess-up ball mentioned earlier. Practise and refine your team's reactions to opposition errors at the line-out, an area of the game that is notorious for mistakes. If you were to fall on and claim 75 per cent of line-out mistakes in every game, you would probably win the line-out stats each week. So build in errors at training and do not allow your front man to turn his rear end to the touch-line: he should be watching the throw and the line-out at the same time. On the opposition ball he can turn fully to the line-out only when he ascertains that they are not throwing to their front man, and on his own team's throw-in he should be ready for a pass from his own thrower-in if his opposite number is not looking at what

Arms only lift.

is going on at the throw. It is so obvious, yet week after week at all levels of the game you see the front man facing fully infield with his hands on his knees; his hands should be ready to do something and he should be watching the game in front of him before he goes completely to full line-out mode.

A useful ploy that the coach can use to sharpen awareness and peripheral vision at the line-out is to carry a spare ball throughout all line-out practices, and the rule is that this ball becomes the priority over anything else when (and only when) it hits the ground. The coach will occasionally let it drop and the players have to spot that and claim the 'mess-up' ball as their possession. This has to be achieved while they are simultaneously concentrating on the line-out practice, which is not too far removed from what happens in a game. The coach can also dummy the occasional ball so that the fringe players who are not lifting or jumping are forced to concentrate on the line-out as well as the potential glory of winning the loose ball.

CHAPTER 10

KICKING

Kicking the ball becomes part of the game in Midi Rugby (U11 and U12) when the drop kick is used for the restart, and kicking from the hand (though never from the ground) is allowed. The tactical kick starts players thinking about the space above and behind defenders, and a well-placed chip can be enormously beneficial when used against a dominant defence.

Most young players will start kicking a ball around as soon as they can, and the coach will quickly spot who can, and who cannot perform the kick with ease. There is, however, a fun game that will let you watch the kickers in an organized environment, and players of most ages, especially young ones, will enjoy it.

Kicking Baseball

The game is called 'kicking baseball'. A pitch is marked out with cones, and bases marked as 1, 2, 3 and home base, which is where the kick takes place. There needs to be a line in front of the kicking area, and no defender is

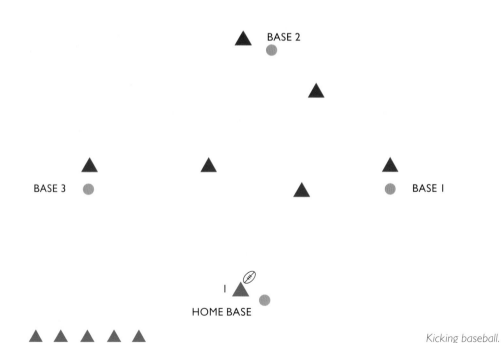

Kicking baseball.

allowed in there; this stops the fielders getting in the way of the kicks, and is also a simple safety precaution.

The rules are simple, and are as follows:

- There is a base fielder on all four bases – 1, 2, 3 and home
- The kicking side (strikers) take turns to kick from the hand (punt)
- The ball must make its first bounce in the 90-degree pitch marked by cones. (You can make up a maximum number of attempts allowed before the kicker is deemed to be out.) If the ball's first bounce is outside the 90-degree pitch area, it is a no-strike
- Once a kick is good (that is, a strike in the designated playing area), the kicker then has to run as if he had made a strike in baseball or softball
- A team scores each time a striker gets back to home base
- If he is touched with the ball before he gets to a base, he is out
- If the ball is cleanly caught by a base fielder before the striker gets to the base he is heading for, he is out
- If there is a clean catch by a fielder, the whole side is out
- You can make up various rules, such as one where the whole side is out when three strikers are out

This simple game will soon show you your best kickers, and it makes the players think about where and how they need to place their attempt. Handling skills will allow the fielding side to get runners out, and there is a real need for players to scan the pitch and communicate effectively.

If and when you find a few kickers who are clearly better than average, restrict them to a drop kick and you will find your best restart options.

Kicking Policy

A kicking policy can help a player get out of trouble, and can also be a part of the team's attack. Most kicks from hand in a game tend to be the result of a spur of the moment decision when the ball carrier feels that he is in trouble and has to kick, or the kick can lead to a gain in territory or even to a score.

However, there are strategies that may have to be practised, as long as the players with the required kicking skills are available. These strategies can add to a team's effectiveness, for there are many occasions in a game when getting out of your twenty-two is a priority. Once you decide that you do have the kicker(s) that you need, it is very important that they practise in a structured way. It seems very simple to suggest that you will go long at a certain point in a game, but the appointed kicker needs to be fairly certain that the skill he is about to perform has been used a few times in the previous week's training, and in the weeks before that.

The coach can organize some basic structures that will be relatively straightforward – but I stress, the kick needs practice, and the follow-up or chase must be a regular chore for the whole team. It is essential that strategic kicking is not seen as a one-man job: the other fourteen have a duty to know exactly what is expected of them, and it generally requires running fast after an instant response to the kick. However, they cannot afford to neglect precise instructions regarding who stays well back as a safety precaution if the opponents decide to return the kick immediately. A policy is required, and it will almost certainly require two players who have a decent return kick from hand, so consider leaving back some combination of full back, winger(s) and fly half.

You may have only one or perhaps two kickers who can reliably kick long, so try to ensure that neither chases a long kick in case the opponents immediately kick back long to you. Get another player to work hard to get behind the initial kicker before the ball is kicked, so that he can then chase the kick from an on-side position and work other players on-side who were initially in front of the kicker.

And if you have a kicking plan or policy, it is a good idea to let the rest of the team, especially the forwards, know what is about to happen. There are all sorts of ways to achieve this, but you need to keep it simple, and you could do worse than have a signal with the player's number followed by a position on the pitch where the kick is going to be aimed.

Strategic Kicking Exercise

Split the pitch into four areas (based on the width of the pitch) to signal where the ball is likely to go from the kick: 1, 2, 3 and 4. Start the signal with the letter K, showing a kick, add the intended kicker's number, then finish with a number for the area of the pitch you will be aiming for. For example:

- K 9 4 – a box kick from scrum-half on the right side of the pitch

- K 10 2 – a bomb from the fly half after possession on the left side. (A bomb is a very high kick that has lots of hang time to allow the chasers to get close to it, either to try to collect the ball, or to tackle the catcher)

- K 12 4 – a wiper from the centre (12) after possession on the left. (A wiper is a diagonal kick that resembles a car windscreen wiper that has gone left or right. It tries to get the ball behind the openside winger, and the chase ensues)

When you use the box kick, it must be seen as a means of regaining possession, and not just as a ploy to relieve pressure. It is nearly always carried out on the right, but is perfectly acceptable if the scrum-half is left-footed and/ or can get the precision on the left.

The first requirement is to get height on the ball, and not to send it too far. Your chasing winger should then jump for the ball and try to catch it. If his opponent catches it, he should be tackled and preferably into touch. There should be a pincer movement with a flanker, usually the openside, coming into the ball as well. Then a centre ought to sprint

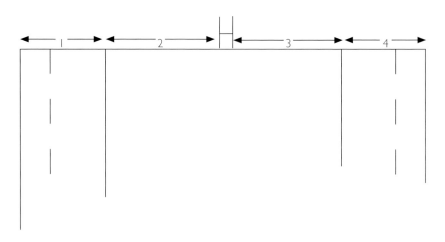

Areas of the pitch for kicking.

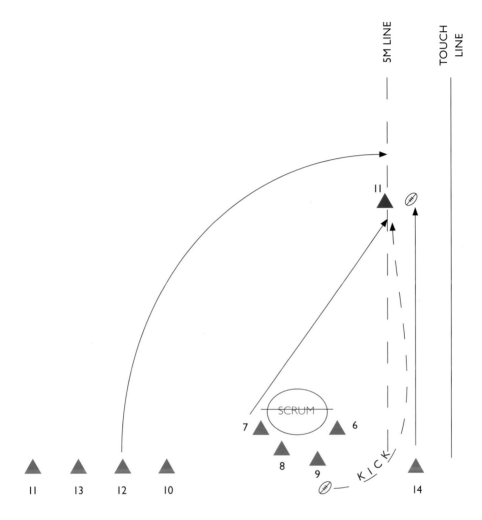

The box kick.

behind their would-be catcher in case he aimlessly taps the ball back. You do not have to follow this formula slavishly, however, and a centre could be part of the pincers, with the 7 going behind where the kick lands.

However, do coach your scrum-half and winger to watch closely what is happening. If their defending winger is well back, why box kick to him? Just pass to your own winger and

let him run into an unguarded area, which will be far more productive than kicking to a man who is already back there and waiting for the ball.

Further Kicking Exercise

The following is a useful game that can be run by the players themselves – and kicking is the key to success. Play on a full pitch with three versus three, and it is a good idea to play your back three players against three others – three of the same team backs, or perhaps the back three from the seconds. There can be a very useful discipline and fitness aspect to the game as well.

- Start the game with a drop kick restart from the 22
- From then on, whoever receives the ball has to kick it from where he received and controlled it
- The choice of kick is entirely at each player's discretion, and the aim is eventually to get to a spot from which a drop or place kick can be employed to score three points
- If the defenders catch the ball before it bounces, they get two kicks, the second of which may be an attempt at goal
- If the kicker kicks straight out, the opposition get possession from where he kicked – unless he kicked from the 22 restart and possession is taken from where the ball went out
- When a kick is being taken, the other two players must get back behind the kicker (fitness and discipline elements)
- The kicking team may not challenge for the ball once they have completed their kick
- Once a score is made or the ball crosses the dead-ball line, the game is restarted from the 22 with a drop kick. If the catchers catch a failed attempt at goal they have two kicks starting on the goal line. If the failed attempt crosses the dead-ball line, the game restarts from the 22 with a drop kick

- You can change the restart points to suit what you want. The number of players can be whatever you want them to be

The game does make players very aware of where spaces are, and where the defenders are standing, and it puts a premium on kicking to space rather than to opponents.

The Dropout Restart

One of the most important kicks in the game is the dropout restart. Most right-footed kickers prefer to kick to their left, but that is a quite difficult ball to catch unless your team has a left-handed catcher. Try to convince your kicker that there is more chance of getting the ball back with a kick to the right – unless you have a left-handed catcher/receiver.

Then there is the dilemma of the not very accurate restart that seems to be taken by the opponents more often than by your team. If this is the case, think about a long restart with an effective chase by five or six players across the pitch. This tactic might gain more than a short restart and it does have some merit, because if the opponents run the long ball back to score, they would almost certainly have scored from the shorter restart kick.

If the short restart kick is inaccurate it is as well to set up practice sessions with the kicker, and to avoid having a session where the forwards chase for any length of time; they just become very tired and exceptionally disheartened. Bring in a chasing/collecting practice period only when you know the kick is reasonably accurate.

DEFENCE

Tackling and defence are very different: the tackle is an individual skill, whereas defence is a group skill that requires team practice, precise instructions on the pitch, and a common knowledge of what happens (that is, who does what) on a clear, concise call.

Defence takes up roughly 50 per cent of rugby game time, so it is well worth developing the concepts and required skills as early as possible. The coach can make all players aware of defence right from the earliest fun games by stressing the first important skill of staying inside the ball. You might have to walk players through a few scenarios to get this across, but it will be well worth the time spent if those players appreciate this as soon as possible.

In a game of touch you are usually trying to develop handling and running skills, but it might pay dividends later if you spend some time organizing the defence, rather than allowing a scattered mess of players who are probably just waiting for their turn to get the ball. If you adopt the refereed game of touch as described in Chapter 4, practising various shapes of defensive patterns can be tried so that the players get a picture of the shape of the different methods.

The team's different forms of defence need to be learned, and it is well worth using the same systems throughout the club so that any player brought into a team knows what his role will be. The key to defence, after players knowing the structure, consists of the following factors:

- Common knowledge of the defensive system(s)
- An attitude within the team that there will be go-forward in defence
- Verbal, confident communication at all times
- Discipline – do not give penalties away
- Reaction to correct the situation if something goes wrong

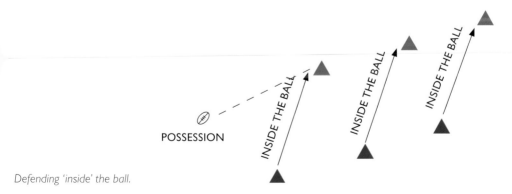

Defending 'inside' the ball.

Players tend to have a very focused, aggressive attitude when they are defending their own goal line, and the coach needs to develop this in the team all over the pitch, as many players 'switch off' when the game is away from what they perceive as the danger area.

Once the ball is out and away from the set piece, there are various ways to defend. The main ones are known as 'up and out – the drift or slide'; 'up and in – man on man or blitz'; 'up and hold'; and 'the banana, or outside man up first'. There is also defence from the scrum and from the line-out, and defence at the tackle.

Up and Out – the Drift or Slide

In this tactic, the first defensive call and movement comes from the first man, usually 10. The whole line moves together (though the openside winger may hang back a little to suggest to the attack that their kick, if it comes, will be covered), each defender taking a line on the inside shoulder of his opposite number.

Once their first man passes, the defending 10 can call the slide – but only if he feels that everybody has time to react and achieve that! If the attack plays the ball close to the defenders, there will be insufficient time for a slide, and a blitz will have to be called mid-way through the plans. This must be practised so that the distances are understood.

Finally all players push one out, hoping to force the attack to move laterally and run out of space with a poor running line.

There are dangers in this system, however, not least if the man who calls the slide does so because he thinks his opposite number is going to pass. He must see the ball leave his hands before any slide is called.

There could be confusion if the attack manages to bring a player on a short ball (to cut it) on to the inside and weak shoulder of a defender. There has to be a player, usually the scrum half, who tracks across the pitch just behind his own defensive line, while staying just inside the ball at all times.

The word 'drift' does not adequately suggest what is required, as there is a suggestion of laziness. The system requires an aggressive one-out push, so it may be best to name it 'the slide' right from the beginning.

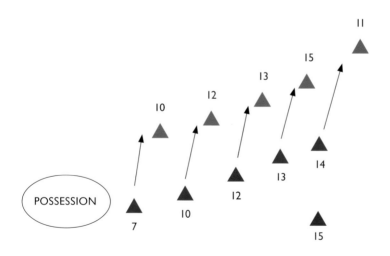

The drift defence.

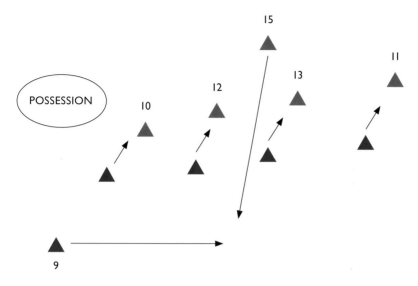

Scrum-half cover.

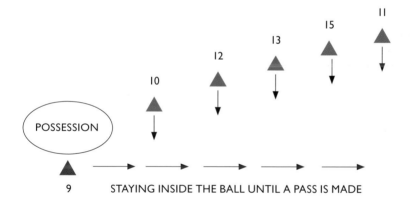

STAYING INSIDE THE BALL UNTIL A PASS IS MADE

Scrum-half staying inside the ball.

Up and In – Man on Man or Blitz

The defenders stand a bit wider than in the slide defence; the outside shoulder of the target is a useful guide. Once the call is made to go, the line moves up very quickly and aggressively to push the attacking line back slightly to where the ball came from.

This defence almost dares the attack to try their handling under pressure as they are deprived of time and space. If the weather is very windy and/or wet, this can be extremely

143

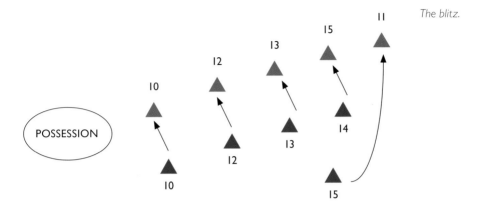

The blitz.

effective and the attack may be worried into an early kick.

Up and Hold

This form of defence is not as aggressive or 'in your face' as the blitz. The defenders move up together and flat against their opponents to show a wall of well organized defence.

There must be a common pace and the line has to be maintained, even when the opposition attempt dummy runners and decoys. If one player does not hold the line, a dog-leg will appear and a space will be left for the attack to exploit.

The Banana – or Outside Man up First

This is a system that coaches and players will see in the professional game. The first forward movement is initiated from the outside centre and the defence takes that cue. All defenders cut back slightly in this intimidating ploy, and it can put pressure on the early ball-carriers when they look up and see the wide defenders further up than is usual. Those attackers, particularly in wet and/or windy conditions, probably have to stay deep to get their passes in, and this can allow the defence to get in with a tackle behind where the possession started.

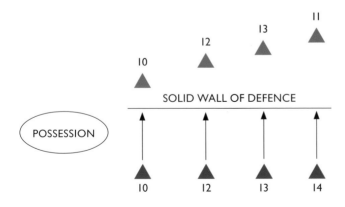

Up and hold.

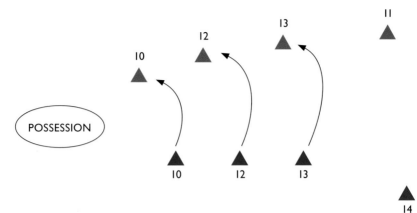

Banana defence.

10, 12 and 13 go up quickly, with 13 leading the movement. The winger hangs back in case the attacking side is forced to kick.

Tackles are made with the inside shoulder (left in this diagram), which will feel strange to players until they get used to it. They must stay outside their opposite number at all times.

However, there are potential problems:

• If the defensive shape is lost, inside spaces become available for the attack

• It can be vulnerable to a grubber kick or 'dink' behind the defence
• At times it looks offside and your referee may penalize it even when it is legitimate
• It requires a great deal of practice, and the time spent on perfecting it may not be worth it when you have so little time to cover other aspects in training time

On balance, the safest options would be the blitz and the slide. There are no hard and fast rules on when to use either, but a

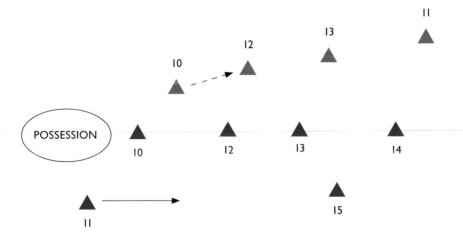

Back three defenders.

useful guideline might be to blitz in both 22 areas and slide everywhere else. Whatever is decided must take account of what the players are capable of.

When coaching defence, work on players *not* concentrating on the ball alone. They should watch the ball carrier's feet and hips, and the ball will naturally be in their range of vision.

Whichever system you use, insist on your defence not following the attack man for man; mark spaces, because if the attack introduces an overload on one side of the possession, they are probably just trying to draw the defenders away from where they intend to go.

At all times in defence the back three players (both wingers and full back) must work together so that the full back is not seen as the sole defender. When the attack goes one way, the (probably blindside) other wing must track across to create a back two with the full back.

Once the attack starts to get close to your line, the position of the full back becomes critical. A rough guide is this: the closer they get, the more blindside the full back should take. Who the full back takes on as his man in defence comes down to two options: track his opposite number (full back) and go to tackle him wherever he enters the line; or stay on the outside of the defence, leave the attacking full back to the inside defenders, and take the outside player.

All depends on what the players are most comfortable with, but it may be best to start with each player being responsible for his opposite number, and the defending full back stays on the attacking full back – wherever he goes.

There are also strategies at scrum, line-out and tackle that can thwart the intentions of the opposition. The first important thing is to look highly organized and efficient – and

this alone can have a significant impact on any game. There are also ways in which the scrum-half and forwards, especially the open-side flanker, can work with the backs in initiating a strong defence. A player's role may be not to tackle, and simply to track across behind the defensive line – but it will be important to offer such a failsafe system to the main defensive line.

Defence from the Scrum

When there is a scrum on the defence left side, there are various potential scenarios.

The attack passes to the open side:
The defender closest to the opposing 10 is the defending scrum-half, and he should aim to get at the attacking 10 *as soon as the ball leaves 9's hands – but not before.*

He must communicate clearly and work with his own 10. If he can get to the attacking 10, he signals that and the slide can start from that. If he knows he cannot get there, the slide will start from 10.

Because the defending 9 is effectively in front of the forwards, another player must be nominated to track across and always on the inside of the ball. This could be 7 or 8 to cover a line break or a kick through.

The attack goes into the blind side:
When close to the line, 6 will have to go for the first ball carrier. However, if there is enough time and space, he might go wide left and leave 8 to come in on the inside. If this is the scenario, 6 needs to hold a little and not rush in so that his 8 can get into position.

If the scrum develops a wheel with the right side up (something the attack are probably trying to achieve), the 6 must tackle the first man as his 8 will have been twisted away from any effective contribution.

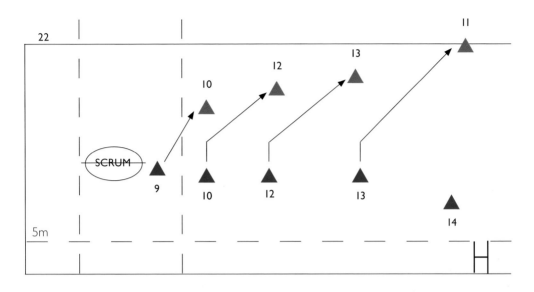

Scrum defence.

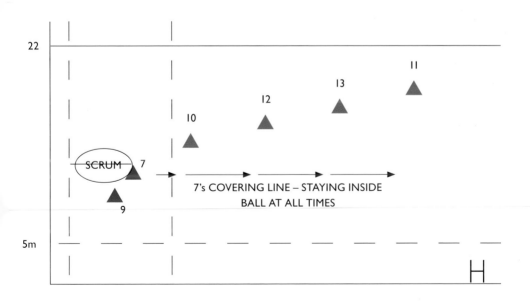

Scrum defence cover with seven.

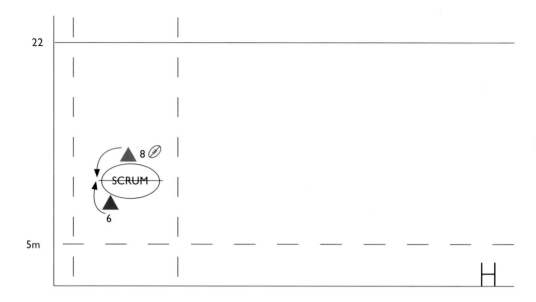

Defending blindside attack close to own line.

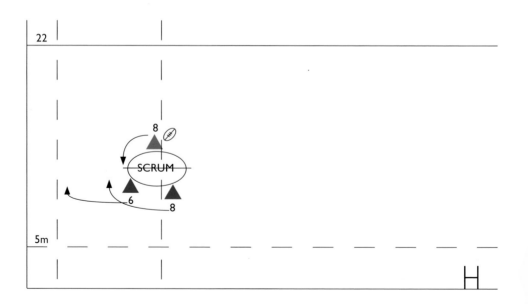

Defending blindside attack with more width.

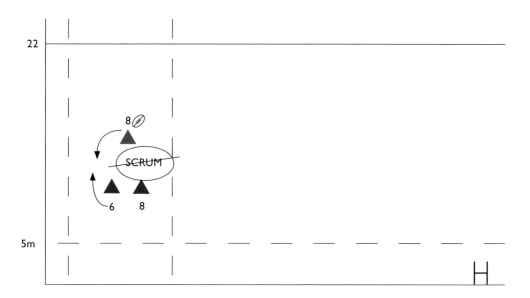

Defending wheeled scrum right.

Defence from the Line-out

The simplest way to defend would be as in the diagram overleaf.

The hooker (2) stays out of any contact and patrols the front of the line-out.

The openside (7) stays at the back of the line-out and starts the defence on to the attacking 10 as soon as the ball is passed.

The defending 10 goes at his opposite number as well, and he calls the start of whichever system is to be used.

There may be a better system by having a completely different defensive line-out where 9 takes the hooker's role at the front, the hooker lifts at the back, and 7 is free to initiate the defence when the ball is passed. This allows your (probably) best defender, 7, to be free from the lineout and closer to the attack than any of the backs.

Defence at the Tackle

At the tackle, there has to be a priority list of what can be done.

First, the ball carrier must try to pass, step around the defender, or play out of contact. If he is held and standing, the next immediate player should try to latch on the ball by leading with elbow and shoulder after the ball carrier has done his best to present the ball at a height that invites that next player in at an effective height.

If the ball carrier is tackled to the ground, the nearest support player should try to lift the ball. The key word is 'lift' so that the player is in a strong position.

He has the option then of 'pick and go', or of popping the ball to another player before a contest for possession begins.

If there is a body (or bodies) in the way, the

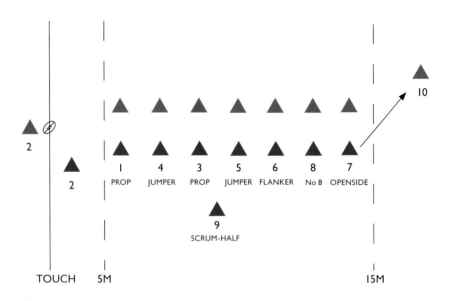

Line-out defence.

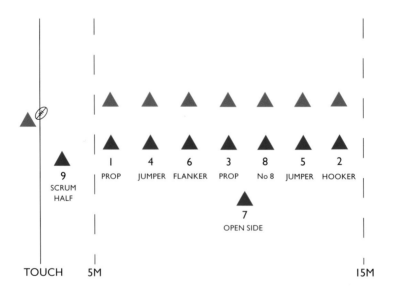

Variation on lineout defence.

Support at tackle.

Lift ball at tackle.

Leaning over to win the ball at tackle.

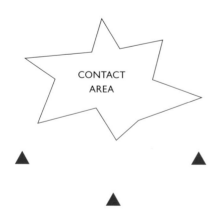

first player should lean over, rest his elbows on the player on the ground, and try to bring the ball back to his side.

If the opponents are gathering near the ball and it can't be played by hand, a mini ruck of two players (sometimes it has to be one) can either bind, go over the ball and protect it by dominating the space in front of it, or drive over the ball together.

Defending vulnerable areas at contest/breakdown.

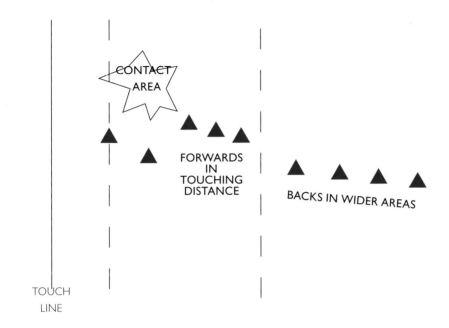

Wider defence after contest/breakdown.

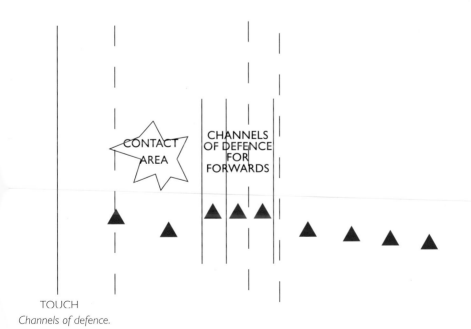

Channels of defence.

If the contest for the ball is turned over or it cannot be won, there has to be a structure to guard against what might happen next.

There have to be three players to protect the most vulnerable areas (see the diagram on page 152).

Then the sides of the defence are built up, especially on the open side. The forwards can provide the first three defenders, but it is advisable to employ backs after that in case the opposition pass wide.

Keep the forwards close together – they should be no wider apart than being able to touch the nearest player's outstretched hand.

Have a maximum of three forwards defending the tackle area on any side. The forwards defend channels, and do not move out of their individual channel for any play from the attack. There could be a pass back, but this will be easily covered if the channels are guarded.

Some players may not be used to resting their bodyweight on another player to lean over the tackle area and win the ball. This skill can be practised by using a large tackle bag: the first player approaches the bag, leans over, rests his elbows on the bag if necessary, and plays the ball backwards to his own team. This looks simple, but it is an area of the game where many penalty kicks are conceded, so it is worth spending time on learning precisely how to perform the skill.

At all times, players need to be coached to attempt evasion as a better option to confrontation when they have the ball. When a defender starts to build up to a tackle from the front, he is bound to drop his body's centre of gravity, and that is when a sidestep can pay dividends. At worst it will force an arm tackle rather than a full-on frontal collision, and the attacking side has the initiative. But tackles occur, and all teams require a defensive strategy that has been practised on training nights.

Sausage-bag practice to win the ball at tackle.

CHAPTER 12

COACHING ON MATCH DAY

Coaching on match day goes beyond just playing rugby. You will be in charge of a routine for the day, and your players will benefit enormously if you lay out a code of behaviour that they will pick up very quickly. This might be a routine such as the following:

- Players are encouraged to be prompt as a whole squad. There may be transport issues, but they should all know the time they are *expected* to arrive, and how they should be dressed
- Have a rota of tasks that need to be carried out on match day. This will vary from home to away matches, but the players should feel that they do not simply turn up to play. This applies to pre- and post-match
- Have designated players to meet/greet opponents (and the referee if you have one from outside the club) at your home ground; and after the game ensure that your players take them to the changing rooms/refreshments
- Insist on all your players shaking hands with opponents and referee after the game, and thank them all for the match

These things will not happen naturally. Most players, but young ones especially, need some instruction in what is appropriate behaviour, and the sooner the process starts, the better. It will not take long for these little disciplines to happen naturally.

Before the Match

Players do not need complicated match instructions, so try hard to restrict what you say. Pick out two or three key points that require full concentration and attention, and stick to them. You may well have just one coaching point, but that will do more good than an unrealistically long list. If possible, talk about things that have been practised and discussed in the previous week's training; throwing a new item into the mix just before a match could easily lead to confusion.

Do talk to individuals in your pre-match preparations. Many will respond better to a few words of individual advice and encouragement than they might to the blanket 'cover all players' exhortations.

An easily portable white board is a valuable coaching tool. Important coaching points can sometimes be grasped more easily by players from a diagram than from oral explanation, and the simple shapes of an effective diagram can be visualized quickly.

A team run is important, but do insist on the highest levels possible in handling, effective running lines, support and putting things right if an error does occur. Too often 'unopposed' is taken as a session where sloppiness and lack of precision creep in: try your best not to allow that. In this run you are setting the tone for the game, and that tone needs precision and the best possible mindset pre-game.

The whole team run might be preceded by

unit practice, but make sure that any forwards/backs split is timed, and that the players know what they are meant to be practising. A vague lineout practice will probably do no good at all, but if the players know they will go through ten lineouts with the emphasis on an accurate throw to the top of the jump, they might just cope with that.

A few hits on tackle shields can concentrate the mind, but keep it short and tell the players precisely what and how many will be carried out. Develop a system that the players know, so that valuable time is not wasted on sorting out who does what. You are not looking for massive tackles in this – it is really a warm-up, and a bit of mental preparation for the contact to come later.

Just before each and every game starts, send out the message to everybody – make the referee your pal!

During the Match

Once the game does start, encourage players. Rarely, if ever, does a player make an intentional error. Even when things go really badly, the players are probably doing their best at that time and in the prevailing circumstances. If things have gone really badly and you want to talk about the game at half time or when it is over, concentrate on explaining what has gone wrong (and if possible, why) without appearing to blame the team. All players need encouragement, especially when the opponents are better. Try to help and make mental notes on the aspects of the performance that will need attention in coaching and practice, but there must have been some positives, even in a losing performance. Finish with comments on these so that the players get a bit of 'up' rather than a list of things that have been wrong.

Develop a half-time routine and try to stick to it with all levels of players. You know how much time is available, so apportion that time to allow the following:

- Getting the players in a state of readiness to listen
- Listening to what the captain may want to say
- Listening to what the coach wants to get across. There will be a tendency to try to say too much and the message will be lost, so be precise and accurate in what you say

After the Match

At the end of the game it may well be that the opponents were simply too good on the day; coaching may never change that! However, you can challenge your players to improve, but avoid giving them the impression that they are failures. They have just lost a game, yet they will get better with practice, and hopefully, they will have done their level best – and with your help as a coach, all players can improve.

APPENDIX

The following describes the New Rules of Play for Rugby at Under 7, Under 8, Under 9 and Under 11. These have taken the place of the Continuum rules, and were brought in to allow more youngsters to be involved more frequently by touching the ball more often. The main changes are as follows:

Pre June 2013	New Rules

UNDER 7

7-a-side	4-a-side
Coach allowed on pitch	Referee as coach
Knock-on is penalised	Knock-on is not penalised
Pitch 60m × 30m	Pitch 20m × 12m

UNDER 8

7-a-side	6-a-side
Coach allowed on pitch	Referee as coach
No going to ground	Can go to ground to score
60 × 30m pitch	45 × 25m pitch

UNDER 9

Tackling is the only new element introduced to this age group. However, the tackle is redefined and the intent to tackle is rewarded by stating that a grip on the ball carrier below the armpit can constitute a tackle. The more-confident players will still be able to tackle yet this allows the less-confident youngsters to make a contribution to the team's defence.

9-a-side	7-a-side
Introduction of tackle, ruck, maul, scrum and line-out	Introduction of tackle
	Re-define tackle
60m × 35m pitch	60 × 30 pitch

UNDER 10

9-a-side
Introduction of competitive scrum and
competitive lineout (early specialization)

60 × 35m pitch

8-a-side
Introduction of competition for ball,
mini maul, mini ruck and scrum
(nearest three players)
60 × 35m pitch

UNDER 11

There is an increase in the numbers competing for the ball in ruck and maul.

12-a-side
Introduction of kicking
Five forwards
60 × 43m pitch

9-a-side
Three-player scrum, midi maul,
midi ruck and introduction of kick
60 × 35m pitch

THE EARLIEST AGE AT WHICH PLAYERS ARE ALLOWED TO PERFORM CERTAIN ACTIONS

Take contact (with the ground, tackle, ruck and maul)
U7 & U8: No physical contact and ball must be *placed* over the line to score a try. Players may not dive on the ball.

U9: First permitted contact with the ground when a player may go to ground to score. Introduction of the full tackle + the intention to tackle is rewarded. (A grip on the ball carrier below the armpit may constitute a tackle but swinging a player by the shirt is dangerous play and is penalised.) The tackled ball may not be contested and the tackled player must be allowed to pass or roll the ball away.

U10: Introduction of competition for the ball (mini-ruck and mini-maul) by the ball carrier +1 and the tackler +1 as long as they are on their feet.

U11: 3 player contest for the ball at the tackle by the ball carrier + 2 and the tackler + 2. Players may dive to recover the ball.

U13 & U14: Hand off permitted.

Scrum
At any age-group level, the scrum may not travel more than 1.5m.

U10 & U11: 3 v 3 uncontested scrum (no push or strike by the team defending the scrum is permitted) with three nearest players from each side.

U12: 5 player uncontested scrum.

U12 (schools) & U13 (clubs): 8 man scrum. Power bind may start (2nd row binding between props' legs with outside arms)

Lineout
U10, 11 & 12: No lineout.

U13: Minimum of 2 players in lineout with team throwing in deciding on the maximum number up to 7.

U16, 17 & 18: Lifting allowed, but not below the shorts from behind or below the thighs from the front.

Kicking
U11: Introduction of tactical kicking with grubber (a kick from hand that goes along the ground and can be chased to retain possession), punt and cross kick + restart drop kicks. Fly-hacking the ball on the ground is not permitted.

U13: Kicking the ball on the ground is permitted.

Not all CBs (Constituent Bodies) and schools have adopted the New Rules of Play and coaches will have to follow their club's or school's protocol. All details can be found in the Rugby Football Union Handbook, Appendix 1 (pages 200–235).

INDEX